ASPECTS *of* LIFE

A Natural History of Southern Africa

ASPECTS *of* LIFE

A Natural History of Southern Africa

RICHARD CHAMBERS AND FRANÇOIS ODENDAAL

Authors' Acknowledgements

As we are finishing this book, the filming of the television series is still in production. It is therefore not possible to extend our appreciation to the hundreds of people that have been helpful in providing access to filming sites, helped with logistics, and enlightened us with their often divergent perspectives on the ecological challenges faced by the various biomes. At this stage we would like to express our sincerest thanks to nature organizations throughout the region, including the National Parks Boards of South Africa, Cape Nature Conservation, Eastern Cape Nature Conservation, Fernkloof Nature Reserve, The Cape of Good Hope Nature Reserve, Kirstenbosch Botanical Gardens, Stellenbosch Botanical Gardens, City of Cape Town Parks and Forests, Grootfontein Agricultural College, the Ministry of Environment and Tourism in Namibia, and the Association Nationale pour la gestion des Aires Protegees (ANGAP) in Madagascar. Various development organizations active in that country also deserve our thanks, including CARE MADAGASCAR and the World Wildlife Fund. Many other companies also assisted by allowing us to film their activities or otherwise: British Petroleum, De Beers Consolidated Mines, Alexkor Ltd. We would also like to thank the governments of Botswana, Namibia and Madagascar for permission to film in their beautiful countries.

The individuals that helped us with the project literally run into the hundreds and it would simply be impractical to thank all of them. Yet, a number of them stand out. They include Louis Raubenheimer, Franni and Adam and Patrick at the SABC; Trevor Dearlove, Nic Geldenhuys, Peet Joubert, Henriette Engelbrecht, Fanie van Tonder, Walter Mzazi and Sarel Yssel of the National Parks Board; Dave Reynell of The Department of Water Affairs and Forestry, Knysna; Willem and Flippie Looch, Marie de Jager, Andre Lund and Rose Willis; all the staff at Syncrolink: Peter, Andrew, Steve, Tess, Craig, Grant and Pearl and Alan, and the staff of Intellvision; our camera operators: Sean O'Sullivan, Glen Thomas and Peet Joubert, and finally Claudio Velasquez for some stunning photography.

A great deal of ground was covered in writing the various chapters of the book. Much of the work had to be done under great time pressures so the book could go into print in sufficient time so that its release could coincide with the airing of the television episodes. We, therefore, had to rely heavily on a number of people to review the chapters, often at short notice. They include Dave Reynell, Marcel Kroese, Phil Hockey, Christopher McQuaid, Neil Grange and Jeremy Midgley. Thanks also to the Struik staff: Ilze, Pippa, Janice, Petal, Dean, Maryann and Caroline.

Lastly, the staff of Eco-Africa Environmental Consultants, notably Paul Green and Marcel Kroese deserve a heartfelt thanks for their diligence in guarding over many aspects of both the filming production and the writing of the book.

Struik Publishers (Pty) Ltd
(a member of The Struik Publishing Group (Pty) Ltd)
Cornelis Struik House
80 McKenzie Street
Cape Town 8001

Reg.No: 54/00965/07

First Published in 1996

Text © Richard Chambers and François Odendaal, 1996
Photographs © individual photographers (see below), 1996
© in published edition Struik Publishers, 1996

Publishing Manager: Pippa Parker
Editors: Ilze Bezuidenhout and Peter Joyce
Editorial Assistant: Helena Reid
Design Manager: Petal Palmer
Designer: Dean Pollard
Design Assistant: Lellyn Creamer

Proofreaders: Tessa Kennedy and Hilda Herman
Photo Researcher: Maryann Shaw
Cartography: Caroline Bowie using Mountain High Maps
 TM copyright ©1993 Digital Wisdom

Reproduced by cmyk Prepress
Printed and bound by Tien Wah Press (Pte.) Ltd

ISBN 1 86825 929 3

Front cover: *Leaf-tailed gecko*
Back cover (clockwise from top left): *Forest fungi, Leaf-tailed gecko, Coral cod, Leopard.*
Spine: *African Goshawk*
Inside front flap: *African fish eagle*

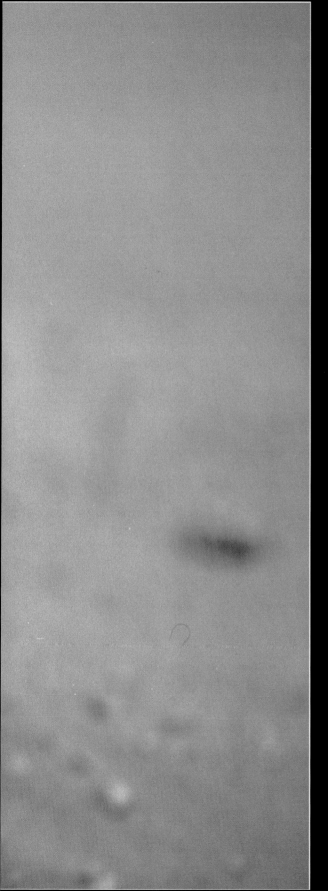

ASPECTS *of* LIFE

A Natural History of Southern Africa

Contents

Introduction

ASPECTS OF LIFE

The natural history of southern Africa is composed of a wide variety of terrestrial and aquatic biomes, ranging

from the vast plains of the savanna to the dark, cold water habitats of the deep

ocean. Many of these biomes grade into one another with no distinct boundaries; others are more clearly defined.

Our cloud-enveloped planet is strikingly distinctive, beautiful, and unruffled. Above its surface, continents and oceans are bathed in an oxygen-rich atmosphere which supports familiar forms of life in an apparently stable system. Yet this impression of constancy is an illusion. This planet is in a state of constant change: its great continental land masses drift across the planet's surface, carried on massive tectonic plates (more than 80 kilometres thick) that lie interlocked over the earth's crust. Sometimes these plates pull apart, forming ocean trenches. At other times, they push together resulting in the rise and fall of mountain ranges. Even extraterrestrial impacts by way of asteroids and comets are thought to have profoundly influenced the history of our planet. Such changes in Earth's history have not only contributed to changing ocean currents and great climatic changes, but have also been the impetus for evolution

within the earth's many varied ecosystems that compose the biosphere. The biosphere, that part of the earth inhabited by living things, can be divided into characteristic regions known as biomes. Each biome is a large and complex ecological unit with its own particular climatic and geological conditions.

Over millions of years, as the communities within these regions become specialised to local conditions – such as climate and geology – plants and animals will evolve in unison to form complex webs of life. What is remarkable about the southern African region is the sheer

---

Above *A thin, fragile layer of atmosphere shelters the earth's many life forms from the cold void of space.*

Left *Our planet has seen many changes during its four-and-a-half-billion year history. One of the most significant has been the process of continental drift which has caused the great landmass of Pangaea to break up and spread across the globe to form the continents as we know them today.*

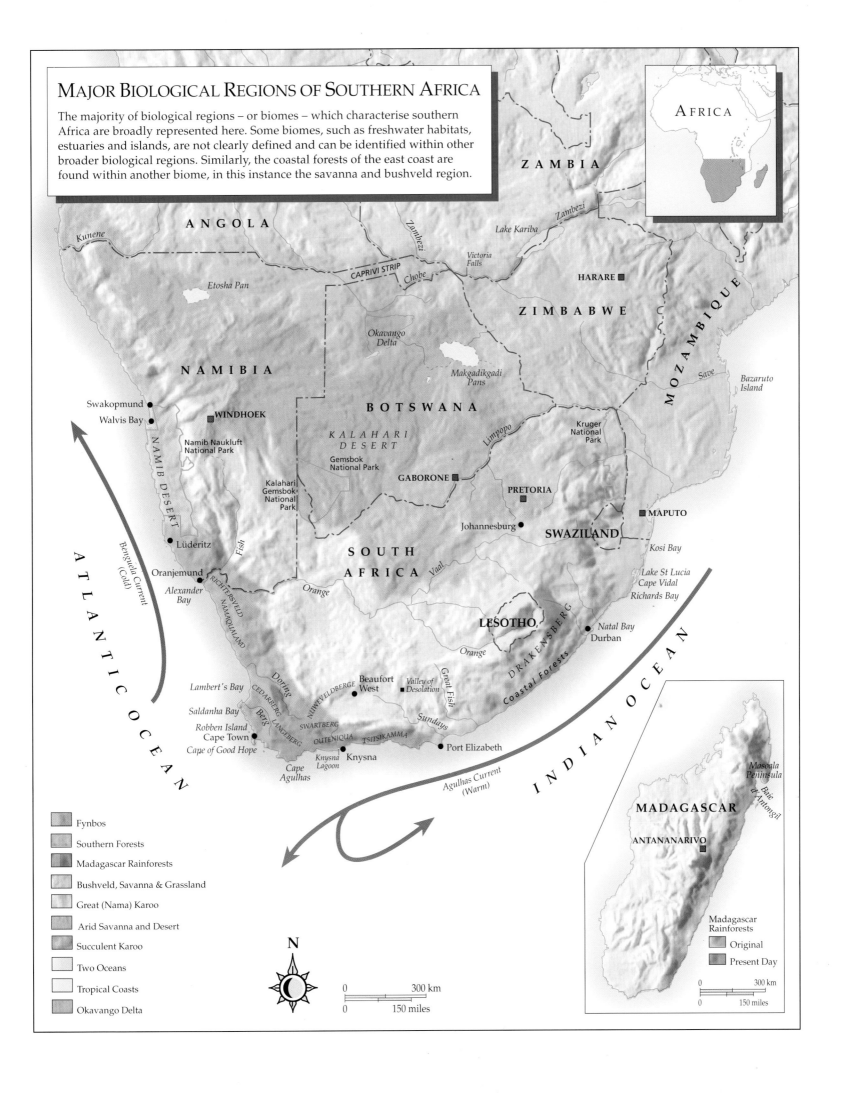

MAJOR BIOLOGICAL REGIONS OF SOUTHERN AFRICA

The majority of biological regions – or biomes – which characterise southern Africa are broadly represented here. Some biomes, such as freshwater habitats, estuaries and islands, are not clearly defined and can be identified within other broader biological regions. Similarly, the coastal forests of the east coast are found within another biome, in this instance the savanna and bushveld region.

AFRICA

ZAMBIA

ANGOLA

Kunene

Zambezi

CAPRIVI STRIP

Chobe

Zambezi

Lake Kariba

Victoria Falls

HARARE ■

Etosha Pan

ZIMBABWE

MOZAMBIQUE

NAMIBIA

Okavango Delta

Makgadikgadi Pans

Save

Bazaruto Island

Swakopmund ●
Walvis Bay ●

BOTSWANA

WINDHOEK ■

KALAHARI DESERT

Namib Naukluft National Park

Gemsbok National Park

Limpopo

Kruger National Park

NAMIB DESERT

Kalahari Gemsbok National Park

GABORONE ■

PRETORIA ■

MAPUTO ■

Benguela Current (Cold)

Fish

SOUTH AFRICA

Johannesburg ●

SWAZILAND

● Lüderitz

Vaal

Kosi Bay

ATLANTIC OCEAN

Oranjemund ●

RICHTERSVELD

Lake St Lucia
Cape Vidal
Richards Bay

Alexander Bay

NAMAQUALAND

Orange

Orange

LESOTHO

DRAKENSBERG

● *Natal Bay*
Durban

Lambert's Bay

Doring

Coastal Forests

Saldanha Bay

CEDARBERG

NUWEVELDBERGE

Beaufort West ●

Valley of Desolation ■

Great Fish

INDIAN OCEAN

Robben Island ●
Cape Town
Cape of Good Hope

BERG

LANGEBERG

SWARTBERG

Sundays

Cape Agulhas

Knysna Lagoon

OUTENIQUA

Knysna ●

TSITSIKAMMA

Port Elizabeth ●

Agulhas Current (Warm)

MADAGASCAR

Masoala Peninsula

Baie d'Antongil

ANTANANARIVO ■

N

Fynbos

Southern Forests

Madagascar Rainforests

Bushveld, Savanna & Grassland

Great (Nama) Karoo

Arid Savanna and Desert

Succulent Karoo

Two Oceans

Tropical Coasts

Okavango Delta

Madagascar Rainforests

Original

Present Day

0   300 km

0   150 miles

0   300 km

0   150 miles

Above left *A supply of clean fresh water, however infrequent it may be, is an essential component of most terrestrial ecosystems.*
Above right *Complex interactions between individual species and the environment form the basis of Earth's ecology.*

diversity of life here. Great forests lie just a mountain range away from semi-deserts; the uniqueness of the fynbos region is unrivalled; and each of the desert biomes has its own particular character, and supports a number of endemic species.

Over time, many species become specialists in their environment. As these species cling – unchanged – to the shrinking habitats in which they have evolved, they find themselves locked into evolutionary pathways that can lead to extinction when circumstances change. Other more generalist species may continue unchanged for millions of years, often having adapted to a wider range of foods and conditions. These generalist species often seed the diversity of the future.

When a small population becomes separated from the remainder of its species group – by a mountain range or a rise in sea level, for example, ideal conditions for the development of a new species arise. Each separate population is then free to follow its own evolutionary pathway under – usually – different selective pressures, while its gene pool remains undiluted by other populations. Given sufficient time, differences between the separate groups can become substantial enough for a new species to be recognised.

Oceanic islands are ideal environments for such developments, evidenced by the fact that many are home to large numbers of species found nowhere else. These are known as endemic species, and every biome has its own collection of endemics. In breaking away from the landmass of mainland Africa, the island of Madagascar has become one of the most spectacular examples of island evolution. After millions of years of isolation from the rest of the world, many of its ancestral species diversified into a biota that is unique to the island.

Similarly, in Africa some five-million years ago the first-known human-like primates evolved. These were the australopithecines of East Africa. Small, slightly built primates , they walked upright among the expanding savannas in a world that was becoming increasingly dry. About two-and-a half-million years ago Africa became even drier. This climatic change was accompanied by widespread dispersal of the hominids and many other animals. Today, several different hominid species can be recognised from the fossil records. Some of these species adapted to the shrinking forests, others took to the savanna and spread throughout the continent and into Europe and Asia.

At about the same time, on the eastern shores of Kenya's Lake Turkana, a human-like primate picked up a stone and, with a few well-aimed strikes, transformed it into a tool. These early tools were used to cut skins and flesh, fashion sticks into spears and dig up roots. No longer dependent on the trees that still provided refuge for their closest relatives, this early human ancestor wandered across the savannas on two legs foraging for roots and vegetables or hunting the abundant game. This species established itself throughout Africa 100 000 years ago. Scientists believe that this early stone-age human was virtually indistinguishable from modern humans. Being of similar brain size and physique, it stood on what must have been the very threshold of humanity.

By 10 000 years ago, what is now recognised as *Homo sapiens* had learned to hunt, trap, kill and even domesticate many of the animals and plants around them. By this time, all other hominid forms, including our close relative, the tool-making *Homo neanderthalis*, or 'Neanderthal Man', had become extinct.

As hunting and cultivation techniques developed, farming communities prospered and, for the first time, humans learnt how to produce a surplus of food. From this surplus grew the foundations of commerce. This step was the key to permanent settlement: specialisation of activities, division of labour, and the growth of the first towns in the world.

Humans were spread thinly across southern Africa because it lacked many of the domestic plants and animals found to the north of the Sahara. They hunted, fished and tilled the land for their most basic needs only. When times were difficult people moved on, sure in the knowledge that there was more elsewhere.

About 1 500 years ago, great commercial empires developed and expanded across the seas, and foreign people started to arrive in southern Africa. But, the permanent settlement by the Dutch on Africa's most southwest peninsula in 1652 marked a watershed in the ecological history of southern Africa.

Over the past 300 years radical advances in technology have made their mark on the land as human society has competed with other forms of life for food and space. The impact that it has had on many of southern Africa's biomes has been immense.

Right *All life originated in the ocean and its vast realms still harbour an unparalleled diversity of life. These barnacles drift in the ocean currents and filter food from the water.* **Below** *At one time the human race was spread thinly across the African continent and for thousands of years lived as hunter-gatherers, in relative harmony with nature.*

The Fossil Plateau

THE GREAT KAROO

Much of southern Africa's south-central interior is covered by the

dry, stony plains of a region that once served as a nursery for emerging life forms. It still has its plants

and animals, but they are far fewer than they were, and their future is bleak.

The Great Karoo, a biological region unique to southern Africa, covers most of the subcontinent's south-central interior (and about two-thirds of South Africa itself) – a vast, semi-arid expanse extending across more than 5 500 square kilometres from the Sundays River in the Eastern Cape to the Cederberg in the west. The towering Swartberg range acts as a barrier, stopping the rains that might otherwise drive in from the south; in the north its fragile soils gradually give way to the deserts of the Kalahari. Its geological deposits date back 300 million years, to a time when the world was devoid of flowers, grasses and mammals. Indeed, they predate the dinosaurs by 50 million years.

A once-swampy, warm land, part of the ancient supercontinent that functioned as a kind of incubator for a myriad evolving life forms, the Karoo was transformed in the course of millions of years into a vast near-desert by geological change, continental drift and great climatic shifts. Today it is a flattish, often featureless place of far horizons, its occasional hills and flat-topped rocky outcrops (or koppies) separated by stony plains. The Great Karoo is not a true desert, though: there is good underground water, and this, together with the sweet, wild grasses of the eastern parts of this region, supports spacious farmsteads and enormous flocks of sheep.

Above *The Karoo sweet thorn (***Acacia karroo***) produces yellow, scented blossoms to attract insects during the summer months.*
Left *A scorpion (genus ***Buthotus***) feeds on a brown locust. Predators such as scorpions are important agents of control, especially in the Karoo where massive swarms of locusts can destroy vegetation over large areas.*
Right *Breathtaking rock formations in the Karoo National Park and the Valley of Desolation are a reminder of a less quiescent earth.*

ORIGINS AND CHANGE

About 250 million years ago great forests covered much of the Northern Hemisphere, while the Southern, by contrast, remained cold and inhospitable to emergent life. Then a radical change occurred: the earth grew warmer, great glaciers melted on the higher lands and a vast, elevated plateau – the original Karoo – became a place of extensive bogs, wetlands and freshwater lakes that were home to the most advanced vertebrates of the time; on land, among the lush undergrowth, ancient tree-like ferns and cycads fed and gave shelter to the ancestors of many modern species. It was here that the progenitors of the first dinosaurs and reptiles evolved from amphibians, most

of them bizarre creatures quite unlike anything one sees today. The rich biological history of these hugely remote times now lies recorded in the geological deposits, and the bones that remain embedded among the rocks have elevated the Karoo to one of the world's top ranking fossil sites.

More changes followed. About 200 million years ago the plateaus were lifted by geological activity, and the bogs and lakes drained away into rivers that gouged deep channels through the terrain, so beginning a process of erosion that continues to this day.

Over time, three major series of rocks were formed. The Ecca, more than 2 000 metres thick in parts, contains coal, fossilised tree stumps and the occasional bone, and dates to the age of the dinosaurs. Below this lies a fossil-rich layer of Beaufort deposits containing the remains of amphibians and reptiles, under which lies the Stormberg series, an ancient foundation which includes the mountains of the Drakensberg range. The legacy of these early times can clearly be seen in the Karoo's many outcrops, extensions of the Beaufort series that are often capped by dolerite – a laval rock forced upwards by powerful geological forces. The dolerite pushed through the cracks in the sediment and spread outwards across the land where, because it was more resistant to erosion, it remained intact while the surrounding sediment washed away.

Opposite, left *When the rains fall, sweet grasses grow throughout the Karoo.*
Opposite, top right *The egg-eating snake (***Dasypeltis scabra***) is able to swallow a bird's egg more than four times the diameter of its head. These snakes have no fangs and are harmless, although their markings mimic those of the poisonous night adder.*
Opposite, bottom right *The rock leguaan (***Varanus exanthematicus***) is one of the Karoo's largest reptiles, growing more than one metre long. It feeds on small mammals, birds and reptiles.*
Right *The black eagle (***Aquila verreauxii***) is one of the Karoo's largest avian predators and also one of the main forms of natural control against rock dassies (***Procavia capensis***) which constitute 90 per cent of its diet.*

THE PLANTS OF THE WILDERNESS

Most of the Karoo receives its rain – between 100 and 150 millimetres a year – during the summer and autumn months. Winters are dry, the days warm and sunny but the nights are invariably bitterly cold with temperatures that may fall well below zero. These extremes, the rapid alternation of frost and thaw, have had a significant erosive effect on the land.

Above *Five species of tortoise are found in the Karoo. The leopard tortoise (**Geochelone pardalis**), featured here, is the largest.*

The rain – when it does arrive – can be torrential, and after millions of years of periodical flooding there is little topsoil left. And this process of desertification continues relentlessly. But despite these unpromising conditions, the Karoo manages to sustain a surprising diversity of plant and animal life. Many of these species are unique in the way they have adapted to the harshness of the environment.

Where giant tree ferns once grew in profusion, there is now Karoo scrub, nondescript flora that is nevertheless nutritious and plays a key role in the Karoo ecosystem. Many plants in this mosaic of dwarf shrubs send taproots down as deep as four metres in search of water.

Despite the sparseness of the cover, the scrub bush is fairly rich in its variety: more than 40 different species have been identified in the open veld. Its few trees and larger bushes are confined to the thornveld, along the many dry watercourses that weave fertile trails across the parched-looking countryside.

ANIMAL LIFE

Again, despite the dryness, the Karoo hosts a variety of mammals, birds and reptiles, and even frog species which are found nowhere else. The herbivores have dwindled in number over time, and some have vanished entirely, largely because so little of the region is formally protected.

Among the most endangered of the subcontinent's mammals is the riverine rabbit (*Bunolagus monticuloris*). An undisturbed riverine habitat provides everything these shy animals need, but water abstraction, the building of dams, and agricultural activities have now damaged these habitats and brought this rabbit, which unlike other rabbits has a very low breeding rate, to the verge of extinction.

Seasonally coordinated behaviour is essential among a high percentage of Karoo animals. As spring arrives, many species emerge from burrows and holes to seek food and water after the dry winter. The intense heat of the summer day, however, forces others into a nocturnal way of life. Reptiles are one of the Karoo's most diverse animal groups: more than 50 species have been recorded. These creatures seek coolness by hiding underground or in the shelter of rocks.

Left *The Karoo's fastest invertebrates are the sunspiders (Family* **Solifugae**). *Their jaws comprise one-third of their body length, but unlike the true spiders to which they are closely related, they have no venomous fangs.*
Below *A springbok (***Antidorcas marsupialis***) can clear three metres with a single leap and can reach great speeds. Only the big cats stand a chance of catching this graceful antelope.*

Many Karoo insects are active at night, filling the air with their calls and chirps; others, able to endure the heat of the day, are active during the early morning or late afternoon. Perhaps surprisingly, many of these insects are black in colour (this increases heat absorption from the sun, but the insects use this solar radiation to their advantage – in order to warm up and find food early in the morning, before the predators become active).

A vital but often overlooked component of many ecological systems, including the Karoo, are termites, whose complex social organisation is based on the division of labour along precise lines. They range far in their quest for food, scouring the veld for vegetable material to take back to the myriad domed nests that dot the landscape.

Grasshoppers, like termites, can also have a profound impact on the Karoo veld, sometimes proliferating into enormous swarms.

When other dinosaur groups became extinct about 65 million years ago, one small lineage, the ancestors of birds, survived and ultimately gave rise to all bird species. Today they are surprisingly diverse in the region and two species are endemic. Large raptors like the black eagle are common and play an important role in maintaining the ecological balance, feeding largely on dassies and similar-sized mammals.

The region's largest bird, the ostrich (*Struthio camelus*), is perhaps among the best adapted: its feathers play a thermoregulatory role by insulating it from the sun's energy, while its catholic diet provides a regular supply of food.

THE CYCLE OF LIFE

As spring warms to summer the dry and dusty land waits patiently for the rains. In the Karoo, precipitation tends to be highly localised – some areas remain thirsty for many months while others, nearby, are drenched by cloudbursts. When this happens, the landscape is swiftly transformed.

Among the strangest of the Karoo's creatures is the tadpole shrimp (*Triops granarius*), which is believed to have existed virtually unchanged for more than 250 million years, its life cycle confined to the temporary rain pools, puddles, drinking holes and pans. Crustaceans rather than amphibians, these animals can complete their cycles and return to dormancy, in the form of dry eggs, within seven days. Their eggs can dry out almost entirely and are able to withstand years without rain.

The reproduction processes of the larger animals are closely tied to the rainfall, and in good years their numbers can grow at an impressive rate. Kudu, black wildebeest, blesbok and reedbuck all find a niche in this vast land. The springbok, though, is the best known of its game animals: these antelope are well adapted to dry regions and require very little water, deriving their moisture mainly from the shrubs on which they feed.

A LAND TRANSFORMED

Today, more than ten million sheep graze on veld with far less topsoil than it had just 200 years ago, when herds of game stretched as far as the eye could see. Stories of massive migrations, known as the 'trekbokken', passing unbroken for several days across the veld bear witness to the impact of man and the power of his rifle. In earlier times cheetah and the Cape lion were the principal predators in the Karoo, but they were relentlessly hunted as settlers from the north (the Bantu-speaking peoples) and later from Europe encroached. Only in the rock paintings of the original Karoo people, the San (Bushmen), can one now see the wildlife that the region used to sustain. The caracal (*Felis caracal*), or rooikat as it is locally known, is one of the last of the surviving carnivores.

The colonial farmers quickly set about slaughtering the indigenous wildlife and pushing the veld to its limits with vast numbers of imported sheep and other livestock. Predators such as caracal and jackal are still thought to take some domestic stock, but hunting and the laying down of poisoned meat by farmers have drastically reduced their numbers.

But it was the fences that had the most destructive impact, restricting the free movement of grazers and disrupting the delicate ecological balance between herbivores and grazed plants. When allowed to roam freely over large areas, the former ate only the most nutritious and palatable shrubs, and pressures on the natural vegetation were never so severe that the rain could not bring recovery. Having evolved over millions of years, the relationship between the land, the vegetation, and the animals was in a state of fine equilibrium. The appearance of the fences changed all this. As the herbivores were restricted to particular areas, so the plants and indeed the land itself began to suffer. The grasses that protected the topsoil were the first casualties. Then, as the more palatable shrubs were overgrazed, all

that remained were the thorny and unpalatable shrubs – and the grazers of this food source, the rhinoceros and elephant, had long since gone.

A FUTURE IN THE BALANCE

It was once said that an ox-wagon travelling from Cape Town to Beaufort West and Graaff-Reinet could be certain to find food, water and grazing all along the way. Can we ever hope for a return to those days?

The problem is that the Karoo's cycles are among the slowest of all of the earth's ecosystems. Man's best efforts must be to reduce the soil erosion and preserve the land for future recovery, which means minimising grazing pressure by adopting new farming methods as well as reducing stock numbers.

Alternative grazing systems are now being tested which attempt to maximise stock numbers scientifically while also conserving the veld, but solutions are not easy to find. An evaluation of the minimum carrying capacity of each farm in the Karoo is needed, as is a careful rotation of stock to create a microcosm of the migrations of the past, and so allow for the recovery of grazed areas.

Opposite *The caracal is one of the most agile of the predatory cats, able to snatch a flying bird from the air. Its attacks on domestic livestock have made it the enemy of Karoo famers.*
Above *Large flocks of merino sheep have become synonymous with the Karoo landscape.*
Below *The Karoo's long history has made it one of the world's most important fossil sites, most noted for its reptile-mammal intermediates.*

Ultimately, though, it must be acknowledged that the Karoo will never support the vast biomass it did a few hundred years ago: the topsoil washed away by periodic flooding will never return. Sadly, much of mankind's impact on this planet is now considered irreversible; sea levels are rising and weather patterns changing. And the future of the Karoo ecosystem, its balance so delicately poised, looks grim.

Outeniqualand

THE SOUTHERN FORESTS

On a narrow coastal plateau at the southernmost reaches of the African

continent lies an isolated forest ecosystem. This ancient relic of Afro-montane forest survives

in an area once known to early settlers as Outeniqualand.

The largest remaining area of Afro-montane forest in southern Africa is bordered in the north by the long shoulder of the Outeniqua mountains, and in the south by the Indian Ocean, warmed here by the Agulhas Current. Because these heavily treed areas are insulated from the harsh, dry African interior by a long mountain chain, coastal weather-fronts drift in and stack up against the rampart, producing what is known as 'relief rainfall' over the coastal plateau. The result is that rain can fall at any time of the year.

ORIGINS AND CLIMATE

The southern forests were once an outlying belt of an ancient, forested region that spread southwards from the tropics. Separated from the equator by vast areas of grassland, savanna and desert, they are now a relic of the time when the earth was a warmer and wetter place. As the African continent slowly drifted northwards and the Antarctic continent settled over the South Pole, new weather patterns were established throughout the Southern Hemisphere and a cooler, drier climate forced the great forests to retreat further and further. In the uniquely favourable conditions of South Africa's southern seaboard these forests were sheltered from the dryness of the interior by

Above *One of the most distinctive forest birds, the famous Knysna lourie (**Tauraco corythaix**), is elusive at times. It has long, opposable claws that grip like hands to the branches, and its green colour provides camouflage. Its full splendour is revealed only when it glides across open spaces to display the brilliant red plumage on the underside of its wings, bringing a flash of colour to the tree tops.*
Left *The sooty blue butterfly (**Lycaena knysna**).*
Right *The fruiting bodies of forest fungi take on an array of colours and shapes. These fungi play an important role in recycling forest nutrients. Many old trees die from fungal infections, however.*

Below *The lichen known as 'old man's beard' adorns the branches of many old trees. Its growth is slow and made possible only in clean air, bearing witness to the great age of its host. Lichens are associations between two elementary life forms: fungi and algae. A jungle of hyphae threads from the fungus supports photosynthetic algae which in turn supply the fungi with sugars and oxygen. The algae also receive protection and gain access to water-borne minerals trapped by the fungi.*

Right *The great yellowwoods are a distinctive feature of the southern Cape forests. These majestic trees tower 45 metres high, emerging above the forest canopy and supported by trunks more than three metres in diameter. They can live to a great age, in some cases up to 800 years. Scientists calculate that the seeds of some of the larger trees would have been germinating at a time when Europeans were still sending crusades to the Holy Land, long before the 'Age of Discovery' had begun.*

the Outeniqua mountains. All that now remains are 60 000 hectares of dense forest, scattered among 900 patches on the south-facing slopes of the coastal escarpment. The largest remaining natural forest, 25 000 hectares in extent, is distributed around the coastal town of Knysna.

CANOPY AND FOREST FLOOR

Most of Africa's rainforests are confined to equatorial regions, where the climate is warm and stable and the rainfall usually high. Southern Africa, by contrast, is largely an arid region with few indigenous forests, though those in the south have something of the appearance of their tropical counterparts.

The great forest trees are the heart of the southern coastal ecological system. Here, there is less species variety than in the tropics: just over 80 different kinds of tree make up the canopy, averaging 25 per hectare. By comparison, an equivalent area of the Amazon jungle may embrace several hundred species.

Yet the two kinds of forest are structurally quite similar: large trees act as the framework within which other plant and animal life thrives. In the soils below, a network of root

systems binds the earth and holds water like a sponge, locking moisture and nutrients into a thin fertile crust. Above the soils, a canopy of intertwining branches and leaves monopolises the sunlight, although some light will always find its way below to the understorey. Here, beneath the canopy, there lies a magical world of more primitive plant species, sustained in lush profusion by the damp environment.

On this forest floor some of the earth's oldest multicellular plants – mosses and lichens, ferns and bracken – find enough light to survive

Left *The underside of a fern frond reveals its reproductive structures. These primitive, non-flowering plants are common in the forest under-storey where they are able to tolerate low light.*
Below *The decaying trunk of a tree supports a host of small invertebrate animals that are dependent on it for food and shelter.*

and flourish, as do the more advanced grasses, shrubs and herbs. The dark green foliage of these plants is very rich in light-absorbing chlorophyll, in order to maximise the meagre rays from above.

Rainfall is relatively high on the southern seaboard – relative to neighbouring regions – but it is much less than that of tropical environments nearer the equator. The Knysna area enjoys an annual rainfall of 550 milli-metres at the coast, a figure that increases to 1 200 millimetres on the southern mountain slopes. By contrast, a tropical jungle in the Amazon basin can experience over three times this amount. Some Columbian rainforests receive as much as 7 000 millimetres in a year.

With their different species and more mod-est rainfall, the southern forests never reach the towering canopy height of their tropical relatives. They seldom rise more than 30 metres above the ground – just two-thirds the height of those in the tropics – but some of their emergent trees, such as the Outeniqua yellowwoods (*Podocarpus falcatus*) and real yellowwoods (*Podocarpus latifolius*), can extend more than 10 metres above the canopy. Both of these forest giants outgrow and outlive other tree species, and both are closely related to coniferous trees, a group that includes the pines and other non-flowering, cone-bearing plants. The larger of the two is the Outeniqua yellowwood. Unlike most other forest trees, yellowwoods bear no flowers to attract insects and birds, but rely instead on the wind to spread their pollen. Less common than the real yellowwood, the Outeniquas are scattered across the forest, their great height a distinct asset in the wind-dispersal of their pollen.

A mosaic of other trees – beech, hard pear, stinkwood, ironwood, white pear, white elder, assegai and younger yellowwoods among them – combines to create the actual forest canopy. Here, wind is a less effective agent of pollen distribution, and many of these species depend on birds and insects for pollen dispersal.

Some of these trees weigh many tons and, to be able to grow tall in the light-competitive environment of the canopy, need exceptionally strong trunks, so the evolutionary process has endowed their tissues with a tough, woody material called lignin. The manufacture and

deposition of lignin, which is embedded in the cellulose parts of the plant, is a slow, energy-intensive business, but it does ensure an impressive life span.

Not all forest plants, however, need such lengthy and costly processes to reach the light: many plants have found other ways in which to send their leaves high up into the canopy, while others are superbly adapted to the low light conditions of the understorey. And still others – the lianas and vines – have no need for thick lignified trunks in order to grow tall: they reach for the light above by wrapping themselves around the young saplings of larger trees. As a sapling grows, so the climbing plants make their way upwards.

Epiphytes are plants that live on, but are not parasites of, larger plants – they simply find a niche in the bark and in the clefts of branches of bigger trees, their seeds distributed by the wind and by small animals that climb up into the canopy. Some seeds remain caught in tiny soil microclimates among the trees' bark and branches, where enough debris and moisture have collected to nurture their root growth. Other plants are directly parasitic, burrowing their roots into the vascular systems of their hosts and using their host-plant's nutritious resources for their own growth.

GROWTH AND DECAY

Rainforests are notoriously fragile ecosystems, highly vulnerable to disturbance. This is partly due to their great age, and partly to the shallowness of the soil layer below. The latter is invariably little more than a metre thick, and it lies on an impenetrable base of clay and bedrock so that deep-penetrating taproots cannot develop. Instead, root systems must spread outwards in search of food and water, and as

they creep beneath the forest floor they encounter roots from other neighbouring trees, and intertwine, and bind with them to form a network of underground growth that enables them to support their colossal trunks with buttresses of interlocking timber.

Where water and nutrients are plentiful, space is the only limiting factor, but the nutrient-deficient soils play a more important ecological role in the southern forests, forcing resources to be carefully marshalled and preserved. The sandy soils are low in nitrates and phosphates, and drainage is generally poor throughout the region. Despite the lush appearance of the vegetation, the cycles of growth and decay pass slowly for many of the forest plants.

In these forests, the death of a tree is a significant event. After dominating its site for hundreds of years, a yellowwood will finally weaken, and its great aged limbs die off to fall crashing to the forest floor. Without the thick protection of its bark, its vascular system is exposed to fungi and bacteria, which enter the wounds and assault the tree's natural defenses. Slowly, over decades of battle, the infection gains the upper hand, heart-rot working away at the once-sturdy bole, gradually debilitating the forest veteran until, finally, it no longer has the strength to support the great weight above.

growth is renewed, carbon dioxide is released back to the atmosphere and nutrients are returned to the system.

During favourable periods, hundreds of forest trees spring into bloom simultaneously. Elsewhere, such coordinated reproductive events are usually designed to saturate, as it were, the market for predators. On the poor soil of the southern forests, however, the phenomenon is thought to occur for different reasons: reserves are difficult to accumulate, growth is slow, and flowering must be designed to coincide with the optimum conditions. The weather, soil moisture and season have to be just right to precipitate these events.

THE FIRST ANIMALS

Because nutrients are in such short supply in the southern soils, the region's plants cannot afford any loss to browsing herbivores, so, in many instances, leaves and shoots are packed with secondary, or defensive, plant compounds that render the tissues either unpalatable or indigestible. Thus, there is not much diversity within the southern forest's animal population; seeds and fruits are the only foods on offer, and most of the larger browsers so common in much of the African bush are absent.

However, the bird life is prolific. About 35 to 40 forest species have been recorded (although more can be found on the forest fringes).

As the tree falls, it leaves a gaping hole in the leafy ceiling of the canopy. Rays of sunlight now penetrate through the gap, flooding the forest floor and bringing life and opportunity to the young plants waiting below. The first to fill the gap are not the specialised pioneer species but rather the shade-bearing saplings that comprise the canopy, for in the southern forests only small gaps open up, which do not promote quick colonisation.

Over many months, years and even decades, small invertebrates, fungi and micro-organisms work away at the fallen timber on the damp forest floor, the tissue-building process of plant

Black Forest Stream

A blackwater forest stream carrying dissolved tannins and humic acids from decaying leaf litter winds its way across the forest floor. Secondary plant compounds, such as tannins and humic acids, discourage browsing herbivores; these plant compounds are then finally leached from decaying leaves by rainfall to end up in the small brooks and streams that permeate the forest depths. They turn otherwise clear water to brown or even black with humic acids, which are toxic to most freshwater animals. These are known as blackwater streams and are typical of the southern forests. Some fish and amphibians, however, do still survive in this harsh, acidic environment. The red-finned minnow (Pseudobarbus afer), is one of only a very few species which is able to tolerate the acidic freshwater systems of the southern Cape forests.

*Opposite The shy forest bushbuck (**Tragelaphus scriptus**) enjoys browsing and grazing among the rich growth of the forest margins.*
Right and far right *A strangling creeper threatens to choke a young sapling during its own short life span as it struggles to climb towards the light in the canopy above.*
Below *Bright red flowers adorn one of the forest's smaller flowering trees, the wild pomegranate (**Burchellia bubalina**).*

Many of these birds are well camouflaged by the green in their plumage. Because flowers and fruits tend to be small and scarce, many of the birds depend on the invertebrate life that flourishes beneath the canopy. Sometimes, a wide variety of species forage together in 'bird parties', gathering each day to sweep through the trees, disturbing a host of insects, some feeding on those that fly, others scouring the forest floor. It's an extraordinary spectacle, and it is driven by good survival logic: it yields more food than the solitary hunt, and there is safety in numbers – vigilance is enhanced (especially against the feared sparrowhawk) and individual risk reduced.

Despite the low diversity of animal life, the southern forests are still home to a few large herbivorous mammals. Bushbuck seek the depths for cover, but feed at night along its lush fringes; monkeys sweep through the trees, foraging widely and dispersing seeds across great distances. Among the larger mammal predators are spotted cats, genets, caracals, leopards that hunt the buck, bushpigs, and baboons on the rocky slopes of the river valleys. Porcupines, blue duiker and bushpig are usually active in the changing light of dusk and dawn but most of the mammals are nocturnal.

Some of the forest's most important residents live among the rotting bark and leaf litter of the floor. Millipedes, insect larvae, worms and snails contribute to the nutrient cycling process, breaking down larger plant fragments into smaller pieces, which eventually become part of the soil. Bacteria and fungi complete the process.

The famed Knysna elephants, remnant of the once-great Cape herds, have now been reduced to just one reclusive female who pur-

sues a lonely existence in the forest depths. The elusive animal was initially thought to have been a male, and in a recent attempt to revive the population, three females were brought in from the Kruger National Park. They established contact and travelled in the forest together for a short while, but one of the Kruger females later died, probably unable to adjust to the more demanding foraging methods necessary to survival in the forest. The Knysna female then split from the introduced animals, and the two remaining Kruger elephants now follow their own course.

THE HUMAN PRESENCE

Elephants once roamed these forests in great numbers, treading narrow tracks that wound among the thick stems of the great trees, across streams and rivers, through ravines and valleys. These routes provided easy access for the British and Dutch settlers, who were quick to exploit the valuable resources of the region. In a few hundred years, the elephants were slaughtered in their thousands for ivory; the forests were harvested for their timber.

The predecessors of these settlers, the original Khoikhoi inhabitants, made fewer inroads: they collected medicinal herbs and bark, and cut a very modest amount of wood, mainly for the making of spear shafts. Dewberry and assegai are thought to have been the most popular. By contrast, the Dutch and British settlers attacked the forest with all the technology and vigour they could muster, and with no thought for the future.

The first areas to be felled were those of the Western Cape, a long time before the discovery of Outeniqualand's riches. The trees in and around Rondebosch, Kirstenbosch and

Newlands were harvested to produce the beams and planks of Cape Town's first fort and harbour jetty. These tiny western patches, sheltering beneath the Table Mountain range, were quickly exhausted, and as the population of the Cape colony grew so the demand for timber intensified, and the swathe of destruction advanced eastward towards Swellendam – where the larger forest tracts began – and Mossel Bay on the coast. Later came the Great Trek – the colonisation of the interior – as well as an insatiable appetite for stinkwood, hard pear and white pear for the wagon-making industry, and yellowwood for use inside the homesteads. Later still, rapid

industrialisation brought new pressures to bear on a now fast-dwindling resource as yet more trees were felled for pit-props, telegraph poles and railway sleepers. Finally, in 1939, conservation laws were passed, and many of the bare areas were planted with pines and eucalyptus. The fynbos of the drier slopes was cleared for yet more plantations, and today the coastal plateau meets most of southern Africa's wood pulp needs. What was left of the old forests was thereafter strictly protected, the few remaining pockets began to recover, and, from the 1960s, the natural forests could be harvested once more, though on a limited and highly controlled basis.

The modern forestry authorities have developed an intelligent harvesting strategy. Only the old and weakening trees are selected for felling, the upper branches cut down and allowed to lie rotting on the forest floor (if left

Above *Buttress roots spread as a wide inter-locking net across the thin soils of the forest floor.*
Left *The* onderbos *is a relative of the European witchhazel and plays an important role in the forest understorey by trapping moisture among the tiny hairs that cover the underside of its leaves.*

where they were, the branches would cause heavy casualties among smaller neighbours as the tree toppled). The tree is then felled and the log cut into sections which are marked for collection. Strong draft horses drag these to the edges of tracks where tractors, specially designed to minimise damage to the shallow, delicate root systems of the trees, haul the loads away. The timber is auctioned and finds its way to a variety of local craft industries. Yellowwood, once used for floorboards, ceilings and structural supports, is now prized as a furniture material, as are stinkwood, white pear and red and white alder.

With so little of the forest remaining, our stewardship of these forests, and the delicate ecosystems they support, is becoming more important: they are among the subcontinent's last remaining pristine areas, and if we value our priceless natural heritage it is vital that we ensure their survival for the future.

Right *Valuable logs are stacked in the forest before being hauled away for auction. The wood is highly prized and sells at very high prices.*
Below *Today, pine and eucalyptus plantations stand in place of large areas of indigenous forest in the southern Cape. The timber they provide is an essential alternative to the slow-growing indigenous timbers of the southern forests.*

Tidal Lands

ESTUARIES

As the meeting place of river and ocean, an estuary is a unique complex, driven by two

major forces: freshwater inflow from the river's upstream reaches,

and the ebb and flow of the ocean's tides, which together create a dynamic ecosystem.

Much of the southern African subcontinent is semi-arid terrain that receives low and markedly seasonal rainfall. In the winter months many of its rivers are either reduced to a trickle or dry up altogether – a pattern that has wide-ranging effects on the nature of the estuaries.

Rivers ending in closed mouths (these are known as blind estuaries) connect with the sea only on a seasonal basis: for most of the time the two are separated by a sandbar deposited in the mouth by wave action and by what is known as longshore drift. But when there are good rains in the catchment area, floods sweep down, scouring the river banks and opening the mouth, pushing vast deposits of silt into the open ocean. Periodic flooding is thus essential in order to open an estuary, converting it for a time into a freshwater system. The sudden change, though, creates new problems for the environment's living forms.

The combination of a river flowing outwards and the daily surge of the tide pushing a wedge of ocean water upstream constantly alters the levels of salinity, and only those plants that have adapted physiologically can survive these shifts.

Animals, being more mobile, use a variety strategies to cope with the dramatically changing conditions. Juvenile fish, which take refuge in the safety of estuarine shallows, migrate during floods. The reward for these survival efforts is a habitat immensely rich in food resources.

Above *A small group of pied kingfishers (***Ceryle rudis***) finds an old boat a useful perch in between fishing.*
Left *The malachite kingfisher (***Alcedo cristata***) with its striking plumage is one of the most beautiful estuarine birds.*
Right *The southern African continent is not rich in estuarine environments; of the 289 rivers entering the sea along the coast of South Africa, only 37 are permanently open, such as the St Lucia system featured here.*

THE ESTUARINE FOOD WEB

The key element in this highly productive environment is the vast input of the earth's natural fertilisers. Many nutrients, washed out from the soil by the rains, are brought downriver to enrich the estuary, and changing tides distribute and resuspend these nutrients and food particles in the water on a daily basis.

The first link in the food chain is occupied by two sources: tiny algae, known as phytoplankton, and the primitive, land-based, salt-tolerant plants of the intertidal areas. Both harness energy from the sun, but because most phytoplankton are often swept out to sea and sometimes suffocated by silt, it is the salt-tolerant plants that contribute most of the organic material to the food web. There is little vegetation in the estuarine system: the majority of plants die off to decompose into organic particles, which form the detrital part of the chain.

Scientific studies reveal that estuaries rank above intensively farmed land, coral reefs and kelp beds as the most productive habitats.

Despite the saltiness of the river-mouth water, marine seaweeds are rare because most of these plants need a firm substrate to which they can attach themselves. A more common sight around the edges of estuarine lagoons are the many salt-tolerant plants, species that often form expansive marshes in the intertidal zone. Other such plants – the succulent marshweeds, *Chenola* (soutbossie) and *Sarcoconia* – grow towards the highest reaches of the tide. Like their terrestrial relatives, these are rooted species that become submerged only during spring high tides. Further down on the shore is another rooted plant, *Spartina*, which forms a grassy plain that is covered by the tide for a longer period.

Upstream, where salinity levels are often lower, the estuary takes on a different character, and embraces a different plant community. Thick banks of rushes and sedges bind the banks with their roots, so stabilising them against the erosive action of floods. The muddy substratum in which they grow plays a crucial role in a nutrient recycling process – vital in

Above left *Much of the southern African continent is a semi-arid area, receiving low and strongly seasonal rainfall. Thus, many rivers only flow as a trickle, or are dry for the largest part of the year. This has far-reaching effects on the estuaries which are supplied by these rivers.* **Above right** *Further downstream, under the influence of the ocean's tides, salinity levels increase, and this river will become an estuary.*

maintaining the system's productivity. Phosphates, carried down the river, are chemically attracted to the mud particles; they become trapped and are absorbed by the root systems of the salt marsh plants, which then secrete the excess phosphates, releasing them back into the water to enrich the system further.

Despite this abundance of nutrition, however, few animals are able to feed directly on estuarine plants. Most of the food reaches them via the vast influx of dead and decaying plant tissue, known as detritus. This organic material is plentiful in most estuarine systems, supporting countless numbers of bacteria. The latter are vital to the food chain because they trigger the decomposition of organic matter and enrich the broth of detritus by adding a vital protein component. This partially decomposed detritus, as well as the dead and dying bacteria, sustain a wealth of small, filter-feeding invertebrates, which provide a further link in the food chain.

ANIMAL VARIETY

The next very important step in the detrital food chain involves many estuarine animals, among them crustaceans, which are each adapted in their own specific way for survival. *Sesarma* crabs, abundant in the many intertidal reaches, are an essential component in the recycling of nutrients because, although they are small and their individual actions do not amount to much, their sheer weight of numbers has a powerful effect on the functioning of the detrital food web.

For those creatures which find food during low tide, water loss becomes a problem since they are primarily adapted for breathing below the surface. Needing a constant supply of water for respiration, many kinds of saltmarsh crabs have evolved water-absorbent hairs on their legs, which trap a thin film of moisture that is then circulated over the gills.

A great many animals, such as bloodworms, sand prawns, mud prawns and saltmarsh crabs, burrow into the sediment (which helps them

Below and right *Salt-tolerant plants such as the succulent marshweeds,* **Sarcoconia** *and* **Chenola** *(soutbossie), grow towards the highest reaches of the tide.*

Left *Burrowing in the sediment is a way to escape predators, and gives access to an environment rich in food. Animals, such as bloodworms, mud prawns, sand prawns and saltmarsh crabs, live and feed in the productive intertidal ranges of the estuarine salt marshes.*

with the many invertebrates, are an important link in the food chain, passing the energy from primary production up to the next level.

Higher up the chain are the birds, aquatic species that feed in large numbers on the abundant animal life, and employ various techniques to sift, sieve and pick out tiny invertebrates. Southern Africa's estuarine wetlands have a splendid variety of migratory species. A spectacular sight is a flock of flamingos, among the oldest of the bird families: fossil records dating back 50 million years have been recorded. Two species, the lesser (*Phoenicopterus minor*) and the greater flamingo (*P. ruber*), are found on the subcontinent; each has its specially adapted feeding method.

Many wading birds migrate over immense distances to reach these wetlands. Some, such as the curlew and sanderling, breed thousands of miles away – as far as Siberia and Greenland and other distant parts of the Northern Hemisphere; for others, like the flamingos, East Africa is the northern limit of their range.

Because of this very critical dependence on greatly separated resources, and on resting grounds during the long migratory journeys, an

avoid predators) and live and feed entirely in the intertidal range of the estuarine salt marshes, surviving safely on the bacterial 'soup' that surrounds them.

Many marine species dwell in the deeper channels, filter-feeding on the highly nutritious water particles drifting down from the surface above. Sea slugs, anemones, fan worms and even barnacles spread their tentacles, hairs, legs and tubes to sieve out nutrients from the

circulating organic matter. Shelled animals such as mussels, clams and oysters feed in the same way – and have an added capability: by sealing their shells, they can isolate their body tissue from the surrounding water for many days when freshwater periodically inundates the habitat.

Detritus is the main food source for most estuarine fish, and especially for the ever-present estuarine mullet. These fish, together

The Common Mud Prawn

The most common estuarine crustacean is the mud prawn (Upogebia africana). Like the bloodworm, the mud prawn forms a U-shaped burrow, and circulates the water (which it has to do in order to breathe and feed) by beating its rear appendages, or pleopods. The rapid movement of these highly specialised limbs ensures that a regular supply of oxygen-rich water reaches not only the gills, but also the bacteria living in the substrate. The mud prawn also uses the hair-like projections on its many mouth appendages to filter out nutritious particles and bacteria from the water-column. Its diet is further enriched by the digestion of symbiotic bacteria that live in its own gut.

international agreement has been negotiated and is now in operation. The Ramsar Convention, one of the few international covenants designed to preserve a particular type of ecosystem, recognises the immense threats posed to wetlands worldwide. It protects several of southern Africa's estuarine complexes.

MANGROVE SWAMPS

The only trees that have adapted to the salty tidal waters are the mangroves, found in some of the warmer subtropical estuaries and forming the basis of the mangrove swamps that start at the former Transkei region's famed Wild Coast and extend northwards towards the equator. These trees have to overcome two major problems in order to survive: first, they must compensate for the suffocation of their roots in soil that is waterlogged and deprived of oxygen (the root systems, like the leaves of plants, need air to breathe). Many trees have developed aerial roots – ones that protrude into the air above. In other instances, the trunk is raised from the ground on strut-like roots that are exposed at low tides, an arrangement

that helps stabilise the tree. The mangrove's second problem is the large amount of salt absorbed by its roots. As the water evaporates from the leaves, toxins build up in the tissues, and to overcome this some mangroves have developed roots and leaves that excrete the salts. Others dispose of the accumulations by periodically shedding their leaves.

Mangrove seeds face a different set of challenges in the estuarine environment: they must be able to take root and recolonise the adult habitat before being washed away. A variety of adaptations have evolved: most of the plants bear seeds that begin to germinate before being released from the tree. When shed, seeds have already developed long, pointed, robust root tips which become embedded in the muddy substrate below.

Finally, mangrove swamps are especially vulnerable to the depositing of silt, which can suffocate the root systems, and to the damming of water in the catchment area, which reduces freshwater supplies and dries up the estuary's banks. These highly specialised trees can only survive in permanently open systems, where their adaptations to the ebb and flow of the

tides allow them to occupy an environmental niche and to compete successfully with their land-based rivals. And it is essential for the health of the ecosystem that they do occupy that niche. Their ability to trap silt, for instance, protects the coral reefs that often lie beyond the tropical estuary's mouth. But large-

Below left The technique by which the lesser flamingo sieves out microscopic invertebrates from shallow waters resembles that of the filter-feeding great baleen whales. Their beaks are curved, which allows even opening along the length, while combs of fine hair trap food.
Bottom right *Marine snails, common in mangrove swamps, live and feed on the trunks of mangrove trees. They are vulnerable to predation when submerged. Therefore, they climb up high on the mangrove tree, to sit in a dormant state, and feed only during the low neap tides.*
Below right *The mudskipper (**Periophthalmus sobrinus**) is one of a few amphibious fish. Its ability to store water in pouches around its gills enables it to breathe on land. An agile creature, it clambers over the mud to hunt for prey.*

scale deforestation in the catchment areas is loading mangrove swamps beyond their silt-containing capacity, and smothering the root systems. And because the mangrove forests are dying, the coastal environment is enjoying less and less protection.

Mammals are quite rare in most estuarine habitats, although reedbuck and otter can occasionally be found where the banks have a very good cover; and hippopotamuses feed around some of the subcontinent's subtropical estuaries.

Below *The curlew sandpiper (***Calidris ferruginea***) is one of South Africa's commonest waders. Young birds spend their first winter in southern Africa until they are sexually mature; they then migrate to the Siberian tundra to breed.*
Right *The greater flamingo feeds on submerged estuarine mudflats, treading the muddy bottom in a circular motion and so disturbing the larger invertebrates which rise to the surface. Long legs and a long neck enable it to exploit deeper waters out of the reach of other bird species.*

LIFE CYCLE ADAPTATIONS

Estuarine salt marshes provide important nursery areas for almost 400 species of fish along a coast often lashed by violent storms. This essential refuge makes an important contribution to marine diversity: submerged grasses provide cover for juveniles during their vulnerable early life; adult fish – marine migrants such as the grunter and stumpnose – search the sediment for invertebrates; leervis and elf, which are specialist predators, feed on the estuary's rich protein reserves.

Estuarine life patterns are both immensely varied and infinitely fascinating. The larvae of the mud prawn leave the lagoon on specific nocturnal ebb tides, and return after a period of development at sea. Reproduction also demands a number of very special adaptations by the largest crustacean in the estuary, the giant mud crab (*Scylla serrata*): the crab's juveniles cannot cope with the changing conditions in their habitat, so the adults migrate out to sea to breed.

Unlike the vast floodplains of many Northern Hemisphere river mouths, a good number of southern African estuaries are in reality drowned river valleys, deep-channelled and also ideal for harbouring ships. Numerous rivers of the southern seaboard rise in the deep kloofs of the Outeniqua mountain range, and pass through the narrow valleys of the upper plateau – an unlikely scenario for the formation of wetlands. But there are two

Above *For centuries the Tonga people who live around Kosi Bay have used traditional methods, such as the erection of wooden kraals, to catch fish. During low tides these kraals trap various estuarine fish, providing an important source of both food and revenue for the local people.*
Left *Titanium mining of the coastal dunes north of Richards Bay is just one of the many threats which now face a large number of southern African estuaries.*

notable exceptions: the Keurbooms and the Knysna rivers both empty into extensive estuarine lagoons, rich with marine life.

Further north, on the Zululand coast, the St Lucia system – largest of southern Africa's estuaries – supports a substantial subsistence fishing community and represents an important local source of income. The villagers harvest its resources with simple fishing baskets that are thrust to the bottom to trap the fish below. In the extensive Kosi Bay estuary, further north, the Tonga people use a different technique, erecting kraals to trap fish in the shallow estuarine waters in the manner of their distant forefathers – the practice has sustained these people for more than half a millennium.

ESTUARIES UNDER THREAT

Siltation is the major threat to South Africa's estuaries. Nutrients leached from the land are carried in the silt and can enrich the lagoon, but large deposits will simply smother it. Silt 'muddies' the water, reduces light penetration, fills up channels and interferes with the process of photosynthesis, which is essential to production at the base of the food chain.

And there are other threats. Urban sprawl in the catchment areas, dams, afforestation, alien invasive plants, agricultural run-off – all have an adverse impact. The capacity of estuaries to absorb floods, mitigating their worst effects and trapping much of their deposits, is overlooked by developers intent on reclaiming the wetlands and detailed scientific investigations are rarely undertaken before work begins. Fragile ecosystems that have evolved over thousands of years of climatic variability now risk destruction almost everywhere.

South Africa's west coast habitats face very different kinds of pressure. The Orange River, which rises in the Drakensberg mountains, drains most of the country's interior on its journey to the Atlantic Ocean, but diamond mining operations towards its mouth need large quantities of water. Moreover, in the arid interior freshwater has become so precious that, with huge demands from industry, agriculture and basic domestic requirements inland, the luxury of allowing freshwater to discharge into the sea is something that can no longer be afforded.

Other disruptive impacts on the estuarine environment are less obvious. Bridges reduce river flow, which upsets the system. Tourism, with its heavy recreational and developmental demands, is adding to the pressures. As more and more people seek to escape the stresses of urban life, the very beauty of estuarine environments has now become their enemy. The capital value of the properties that border estuaries spurs yet more development.

Sixty per cent of the population lives within 60 kilometres of the coastal zone, and this figure is rising steadily. Estuaries are increasingly being denied the essential component of their natural cycle – the normal range of flood events. Small floods are often completely captured by reservoirs and dams; today, over 40 per cent of South Africa's river flow fails even to reach the sea. Much of this water is wasted as it evaporates back into the atmosphere; the remainder supplies an expanding population and its industries. The result is that many estuaries now no longer receive enough water to displace the seasonal sand bars which isolate them from the sea, and are destined to become salty inland lakes.

A detailed scientific conservation programme must be implemented before the ecosystems are further degraded. The exercise should take in not only the estuary itself and the river that feeds it, but also the lands of its catchment, since it is here that the rainwaters begin their journey.

Human association with estuaries goes back a long way – to the very dawn of civilisation. The ancient floodplains of the Nile, Tigris and Euphrates rivers gave sustenance to humankind's first attempts at agriculture, which in turn gave birth to the first great civilisations. However, we are now doing our best to destroy these precious areas with massive

Above *The journey through the Heads on the Knysna Lagoon was not without danger for the many sailing ships that entered in the past; but it never fully developed as a coastal port.*
Below *The rare Knysna seahorse (**Hippocampus capensis**) is one of the estuary's vulnerable animals – a single catastrophic event in this lagoon could spell extinction for this species.*

investment in crop production, drainage, water abstraction and waste disposal. These wetland environments, and the plants and animals that inhabit them, rank among the most threatened in southern Africa. More-over, the predicted rise of the sea level will present greater problems in future. Somehow, the food resources of the world's most productive ecosystems must be preserved, and developed for the growing population.

Long ago human beings understood the profound rhythms of nature and the value of these highly dynamic environments, much as a farmer reads the seasons, but somewhere along the line we have lost touch with nature, and we now risk the annihilation of some of planet earth's most precious habitats.

Land of Fire

THE FYNBOS BIOME

One of the world's most distinctive and diverse botanical regions lies at

the southwestern tip of the African continent. Known as the Cape Floral Kingdom, it encompasses

a remarkable 8 000 and more species of flowering plant.

Fynbos vegetation stretches in a long crescent from the rugged mountains of the Western Cape, near Cape Town, through valleys, mountains and across coastal plains to Grahamstown in the east. Its origins, like much of the world's floral wealth, go back to the supercontinent of Gondwanaland which, more than 100 million years ago, nurtured the first flowering plants. The break-up of this massive landmass into the world's continents – some 40 million years ago – brought with it fundamental, often cataclysmic evolutionary changes. The great dinosaurs, lords of the earth, abruptly disappeared, to be succeeded by the mammals. The earth's dominant flora at the time comprised primitive cone-bearing gymnosperms (literally 'naked seeds') but these, too, were to make way for another form of plant life, one which would spread colour across the face of the planet.

The emergence of these flowering plants, or angiosperms, signalled a significant evolutionary event. Floral reproduction became a more complex process: the angiosperms depended on animal groups (especially insects) and not on the wind for the dispersal of seed and pollen. Many of their early descendants can still be found in the Cape Floral Kingdom.

Fynbos vegetation once extended throughout southern Africa. But as the African continent drifted slowly northwards towards the equator, climatic conditions became warmer and many tropical species of the Afro-montane forests spread into the wetter south, gradually pushing

Right *The early Dutch settlers to the Western Cape called the vegetation here 'fynbos' or fine-bush, a term used to describe the numerous tough, low-growing plants of this floral kingdom – one of the smallest in the world. Members of the Protea family are typical of fynbos vegetation, and produce beautiful floral displays as diverse as* **Protea eximia** *(a true protea)* **(left)** *and pincushion proteas of the* **Leucospermum** *genus* **(above)**.

Above *Heathers (Genus* Erica) *are common in Europe and the Mediterranean, but have their highest concentration in southern Africa; about 600 species occur in the southwestern Cape.*

back the fynbos frontier and, eventually, confining a great many species to a small area centred around the Western Cape.

The southern seaboard's present climate stabilised approximately two and a half million years ago in a typical Mediterranean pattern whose principal features are warm, very dry summers and cool, wet winters; the seasons are punctuated by strong, southerly winds which blow from the South Atlantic Ocean, alternating with the warm, dry berg winds which blow from the hot interior. The changing environ-

ment triggered many specialised adaptations to summer-drought conditions, to poor soils, and to one of the most critical elements of the new ecosystem: periodical veld fires. Today the fynbos biome is characterised by a scarcity of trees, grasses and evergreen succulents; there is mainly a preponderance of small shrub bushes of the protea (Proteaceae) and erica (Ericaceae) families.

The strikingly varied geology of the Western Cape region, in conjunction with the climatic variability and a considerable range of soil types over small distances, has created many ecological niches which, together, embrace a stunning diversity of flowering plants. Some of the best known – the proteas, for instance – are also among the world's oldest. The Proteaceae, one of the four major fynbos groups and

named after the Greek sea-god Proteus, come in a huge number of different forms, but for the most part their flowers are spectacular bouquets comprising as many as a hundred small blooms grouped together, with a garland of equally colourful bracts.

PLANTS AND
ANIMALS IN PARTNERSHIP

Elaborate flowers usually indicate elaborate means of animal pollination, and the blooms of the fynbos are no exception. However, on the southwestern tip of Africa, most animal life is surprisingly impoverished in comparison with the rich profusion of the floral realm.

Insects, typically, comprise most of the diversity and many flowering plants compete

Right *Bontebok were once found in great herds but demand for their skins reduced numbers to just a handful. Saved from extinction by a breeding programme, they now thrive in many fynbos reserves such as the Bontebok Park.*
Below *The green stick insect (**Macynia labiata**), found in fynbos, is one of 50 species of stick insects found in southern Africa. After mating, the larger female lays numerous hard, seed-like eggs that fall to the ground, where they hatch into nymphs during the hot summer months.*

for their pollinating attention with the colour of their blooms and the sweetness of their nectar. This rivalry has been the driving force behind the evolution of the flowering plants generally, and that of fynbos in particular. Bees, beetles, flies and mites can all find year-round sustenance among the wealth of pollen- and nectar-bearing flowers.

In some cases, the plant-insect association has existed for so long that the two have become wholly dependent on each other. The extinction of one kind of plant can also bring about the demise of an entire insect species.

Although Africa is famed for the number and variety of its mammals, few are endemic to fynbos principally because palatable grasses and energy-rich seeds and fruits are scarce. As a result, the carrying capacity is far less than that of other vegetation types.

Baboons and other omnivorous mammals are more common than large grazers and browsers because their major predator, the Cape leopard (*Panthera pardus*), is becoming increasingly rare. Livestock farming and relentless human encroachment have confined this large and lovely cat to just a few mountain ranges, and there too it is still being hunted.

Some large mammals *have* managed to thrive on the hardy vegetation, among them the eland (*Taurotragus oryx*), bontebok (*Damaliscus dorcas*), mountain zebra (*Equus zebra*), and grysbok (*Raphicerus melanotis*). Many of the herbivores concentrate in the coastal areas, or Sandveld, where grazing is moderately good.

The soft, sandy soils of the southwestern Cape are ideal for burrowing, and several species of mole and mole-rat flourish in the coastal fynbos region. The Cape dune mole-rat

(*Bathyergus suillus*) habitually digs tunnels of up to 100 metres long in its quest for bulbs, corms, rhizomes and tubers – the storage organs of many fynbos species. Known as geophytes, these plants make up one of the floral kingdom's major groups. Most of the geophytes have a very limited range, and by collecting their storage organs and storing them in underground larders, the rodents play an important role in plant dispersal. Bulbs are either broken up and moved to larders, where they are occasionally forgotten, or dropped along the way.

A KINGDOM OF DIVERSITY

Some of the best-known fynbos plants belong to the diverse ericoid group, which embraces about 3 000 described species. In southern Africa the family Ericaceae alone totals more than 600. Erica flowers of this group form either open or closed bells, and vary in size from a large six centimetres to the smallness of a pinhead. The flower's length, though, is often perfectly matched by the visiting insects that feed upon it, and the plant's reproductive structures – the anthers and stamens – are so positioned that a bird's beak or an insect will always brush against the same spot, thus ensuring the correct transfer of pollen from one flower to another. Unwanted visitors – insects lacking the correct body structures for pollen transfer – are impeded by a variety of bracts, sepals and sticky hairs. The leaves are small and hard, which reduces water loss; leaf margins are rolled under to protect their respiratory pores from evaporation during the dry summer winds.

Despite this floral diversity, the fynbos supports relatively few bird species compared with other veld types because its fruits, seeds and

Left, above *Orange-breasted sunbirds (***Nectarinia violacea***) spend the winter months feeding on proteas and then move to feed on the spring-flowering* Erica *species. These small birds can often be seen hanging upside-down on the bowl-shaped flower heads of* Leucospermum *plants, probing its nectar reserves from below.*
Left *The Cape sugar bird is endemic to fynbos, and pollinates a wide variety of flowers. This bird is standing on top of a protea flower to feed.*

large insects are limited in their variety. Nectar, however, provides a major attraction, nourishing birds which have a specialised diet. While many proteas flower in winter, other fynbos plants tend to bloom during the spring and summer months – a pattern that ensures a year-round supply to nectar-feeders such as the Cape sugar bird (*Promerops cafer*) and the sunbird species.

The ericas appear to be more specialised in their relationship with these birds – over a 100 *Erica* species rely on sunbirds for pollination; many of them have long, curved flowers that match the length of the sunbirds' beaks, so receiving exclusive attention. But in some cases the pollen itself may be transferred by tiny flower-mites which hitch a lift on the facial feathers of the bird; by doing this, they promote their own dispersal as well as that of the flower's pollen.

*Fires are thought to have a cyclical nature in the fynbos vegetation (**above**) and many plants have thick fire-resistant bark (**right**) to withstand the passing flames. Any area where sufficient fuel has built up after several years of growth is susceptible. This cycle may be as short as five years in some locations, although other areas may persist unburnt for as long as 40 years. The result of a long unburnt period is a reduction in diversity as soil nutrients become scarce and certain species monopolise resources.*

A good number of plant species, though, need no assistance from animals. The third major fynbos plant group, the Restionaceae family, is related to primitive grasses and, as is the case with the grasses, the agents of pollination are the strong winds that blow across the southwestern Cape. These rush-like reedy

The Monkey Beetle

Monkey beetles belong to the Rutelinae family, and are related to scarab beetles (which include dung beetles). Monkey beetles are endemic to southern Africa, and are easily recognisable, often seen protruding from flower heads with only their long limbs and furry bodies visible. Typically, they tunnel deep into the flower heads to feed, their specially adapted hind limbs enabling them to extract themselves when they have had their fill. As they feed, the hairs on the bodies of these highly active creatures trap some of the pollen grains from the flower; in this way the beetles play an important role in the transfer of pollen from flower to flower.

Cape of Good Hope. Vasco da Gama called the land 'terra de fume', or 'land of fire'. Here, however, fire is not the powerfully destructive force one expects but, rather, a vital element in the survival of the diverse and complex ecosystem. Many plants have evolved special adaptations to cope with the frequent bushfires that sweep across the region, and some are even dependent on fire to complete their life cycles. The stems of some are protected by thick, flame-resistant bark; others, such as the restios and geophytes, re-emerge from underground growth after the flames have passed. Essentially, fire sustains floral diversity by preventing the dominance of a few mature species of any one group. The fire unlocks valuable nutrients bound up in the plant tissues, and releases them back into the soil as a fine ash, where they will once again nurture new growth.

While many of the animals that live in the fynbos region have adapted to cope with sweeping veld fires, the periodic burning of countryside has been responsible for their low diversity. Unlike plants, which cannot move, many adaptations are behavioural: animals escape fires by sheltering below ground in hollows and burrows, where the temperature is lower than on the surface, while others seek safety in and around water. The larger ones flee the area in advance of the fire and, when the danger has passed, return, often to exploit the fresh post-fire growth.

Below *The pugnacious ant (**Anoplolepis custodiens***) *plays a critical role in the fynbos ecosystem, transporting seeds to precise levels below the surface in exchange for nutritious seed caps. Temperature is crucial for seed germination and the exact depth beneath the soil must be reached. The ants ensure this and, in return for their rich meal, also ensure that the seeds are safe below the ground from fire and the foraging seed-eaters above.*

plants are entirely diecious – they have separate male and female forms – and occur almost exclusively in the fynbos biome, usually forming dense stands in areas of poor drainage.

FIRE AS A FRIEND

Perhaps the most fitting description of the Cape Floral Kingdom was that recorded by the second European navigator to sail around the

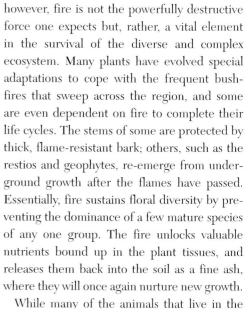

Right Witsenia maura *occurs at just two locations along the Cape Peninsula. It can easily be distinguished by its extraordinary yellow and black flowers that have given it the nickname 'bokmakieries' tail', after the bird with similar tail colours. There are no obvious pollinators for this species, and some believe it was once pollinated by a giant sunbird which has since become extinct.*

The bulbous geophyte plants, with their underground storage organs, are well adapted to cope with fire and are often the very first to sprout after burning (geophytes – which include the familiar lilies, irises and orchids – are much sought after by collectors for their spectacular flowers). Members of the daisy and geranium families also grow in this manner, but many other plants bridge the fire cycles by surviving as seeds.

Here, a whole new range of adaptive traits is linked to fire events: some plants – the proteas for instance – specifically time their seed release to coincide with burning. Old flower-heads dry out after fertilisation and eventually form a cone. In many cases these cones remain on the plant with seeds locked inside until a fire kills the plant. The cone will then open, sometimes as little as a few hours after the fire has passed, to release its entire contents. In other species, seeds lie dormant in the soil for long periods of time, waiting for the next burn before they germinate. One of the mechanisms by which this dormancy is broken was discovered only recently: it was found that smoke, as well as heat and moisture, played an important role; seeds in the soils were cued to germinate by certain smoke gases that permeated the soil.

Some species produce fire-resistant seeds, but for the most part survival is only possible below the ground, where the heat of the fire barely penetrates. One of the most important insects of the fynbos region plays a critical role in this process: ants are ubiquitous in many ecosystems, but one particular species, the pugnacious ant, has an intimate association

Right **Roridula gorgonias** – *one of two members of the Roridulaceae family endemic to the Western Cape. Both species have sticky leaves that ensnare passing insects. The trapped insect is then quickly mobbed by a host of hemipteran beetles (**Pameridae roridulae**) that live only on this plant. Every beetle attempts to pierce the prey with its specially adapted mouthparts, enabling it to suck out the insect's body fluids. In return for this food source, these beetles are thought to reward the host plant by defecating on its leaves, the faeces then fertilising the plant from above ground.*

with as many as 3 000 fynbos plant species. It collects the seeds after they have been released and carries them below to its nest, where it will feed on an oily nutrient-rich cap called an eliosome, usually found at one end of the seed. In some cases the whole seed may be covered by an eliosome, and the ants eat only the surface, leaving the untouched seed behind to germinate.

VARIETY AMONG ADVERSITY

The poor soils of the region have prompted some rather more unusual adaptations. Over three-quarters of the plants of the fynbos have some kind of association with the fungi that grow around their root systems. The fungi absorb nutrients such as phosphorus, calcium and potassium, some of which they exchange for the carbohydrates and shelter provided by the plant's roots. These fungal systems prevent soil-living pathogens from entering the plant; in other cases bacteria grow in association with roots, producing nodules that convert nitrogen from the atmosphere into a form that can be absorbed by the roots.

In a few extreme cases, plants actually function as carnivores; the fynbos region has several species of *Drosera* (sundew plants). In addition to this, it also hosts the world's tallest carnivorous plants, the two species which comprise the family Roridulaceae. Worldwide, in areas where the soils are poor in nitrogen, some species have evolved ways to capture and digest the tissues of insects.

Other endemic fynbos plants are equally strange and just as rare. Many have extremely small ranges, sometimes confined to a single hillside or valley. *Witsenia maura* is one such example: it survives in just a few patches on the Cape Peninsula and at Betty's Bay. Despite its striking yellow and black flowers, the species has no known pollinators, and its only means of reproduction is by asexual growth. Their small ranges make these plants very vulnerable to extinction, and indeed a significant number of fynbos species are Red Data listed. One can only speculate on the number lost before proper records were kept. Many of the region's animals may also face a similar threat, notably reptiles, amphibians and endemic fish species.

Above *The thick, fleshy leaves of many fynbos bushes enable them to withstand the dry summer months and their desiccating winds by reducing surface area and conserving the plant's water supply until the winter rains bring relief and promote new growth.*

Left *The restios are a very distinctive sight among other fynbos plants. Because their tall stems are ideal for the thatches of houses and buildings, a great many areas in the southern Cape are still harvested today for the purpose of supplying roofing material.*

A large variety of lizards, including skinks, agamas and chameleons, live in the fynbos. Although there are no endemic snakes, puff adders (*Bitis arletans*) and Cape cobras (*Naja nivea*) are still common predators of many small mammals and reptiles.

THE THREATENED LAND

For many thousands of years humans lived in balance with the fynbos ecosystem. The original nomadic folk were succeeded by migrant populations from the interior – pastoralists who drove cattle before them. These people, who were known as Hottentots, had an amazing knowledge of the medicinal properties of many of the fynbos herbs: early European settlers reported hundreds of different plants used in the prevention and treatment of sickness. The leaves of the buchu bush, for example, alleviated stomach problems and, when mixed with sheep fat, kept biting insects at bay. Flavourings, oils and perfumes are still, today, extracted from this rich botanical resource. Many plants were collected and sent back to the early taxonomists of Europe. Taxonomy's founding father, the Swedish naturalist Karl Linnaeus, described the Cape as 'paradise on earth'.

In addition to its stunning beauty, the fynbos region has its own economic potential. It supports a substantial cut-flower industry, employing people in rural areas who would otherwise be forced to relocate to urban settlements on the edges of cities. The international trade in proteas alone is worth more than R50 million in foreign currency per annum. The cultivation of rooibos and other varieties of herbal teas is another lucrative industry which is already unable to meet the growing inter-national demand, particularly from Japan and other parts of the Far East.

More than 90 per cent of the lowland fynbos has now been replaced by urban development, agriculture, dams, roads and plantations. Today, with the further development of the Western Cape, this unique biome, like so many times in the past, is once again being pushed to the frontiers of extinction, forced to take refuge in the rugged mountains among which it first evolved.

Above *Over the past two centuries increased human numbers have created serious threats to fynbos, pastures, wheat fields and vineyards having replaced natural habitats. Many plant species with small ranges have been lost forever; many more are now on the brink of extinction, surviving only in the remotest mountain areas.* **Right** *One of five tortoise species found living in the fynbos, the geometric tortoise* (**Psammobates geometricus**) *is the second rarest species in the world, with less than a few thousand remaining.*

Life in the Thirstland

THE SUCCULENT KAROO

The cold Atlantic rollers beat relentlessly against southern Africa's

rugged northwestern coastal region – a desert-like land which offers nothing, it seems,

except sand, scatters of low bushes and the lonely sound of the wind.

The 100 to 150-kilometre-wide coastal strip known as the 'succulent Karoo' spans two countries: South Africa in the south, and Namibia in the north. Bisected by the Orange River, this fascinating desert and semi-desert land embraces different regions, each with its geographical, political or informally evocative name: Namaqualand, the Thirstland, the Sperrgebiet (which means 'forbidden territory'), the Richtersveld, the Garden of the Gods, the Land God Made in Anger, and others.

The succulent Karoo is one of the world's most unusual desert biomes, one where – as the name suggests – succulent plants proliferate, sustained (especially in the west) in their harsh, arid environment by unique weather conditions. Like the adjoining fynbos countryside to the south-west, the region has a strongly seasonal winter rainfall pattern, its cold fronts originating in the south Atlantic. Rainfall varies greatly from area to area, but is never plentiful: precipitation ranges from 300 to a pitiful 20 millimetres a year. The more generous summer rainfall regions of the interior, however, do sometimes bring their influence to bear, so the desert can expect rain on any day of the year. The region also benefits from the heavy coastal fogs that roll in from the cold Atlantic Ocean, great misty mantles which usually dissipate a few kilometres from the shoreline. The valley of the Orange River acts as a channel that carries the fog further inland, spreading precious moisture along its banks.

In the simplest terms, the succulent Karoo's climate is determined by the cold Benguella Current that originates in the icy southern oceans and

Above *The terracotta gazania (***Gazania krebsiana***) bears flowers a full eight centimetres in diameter and is among the region's most beautiful plants.*
Left *The striped sandveld lizard (***Nucras tessellata***) is one of the many lizard species found in the succulent Karoo.*
Opposite *Namaqualand daisies (***Dimorphotheca sinuata***) form part of a spectacular display in Namaqualand, a region within the succulent Karoo.*

Left *The early Khoisan people reputedly used the hollowed-out branches of* **Aloe dichotoma** *as quivers in which to carry their arrows, hence its common name, quiver tree. This plant is not tied to watercourses, as are other trees in the region, and can store most of the water it needs in its fleshy trunk. Its trunk has white reflective bark (**opposite**) so as to minimise water loss.*

flows northwards along the coast. The cold sea air rolls in to meet the warmer, rising air of the land, and condenses to form a fog bank. At other times, hot winds – known as berg winds – blow in from the east, across the dry plains, sand dunes and exposed rock surfaces. They sometimes last for days, shrivelling the plants of the wilderness and consuming precious moisture brought in by the life-giving fogs.

THE SUCCULENT FLORA

The succulent Karoo has lime-rich but shallow soils and is rich in geophytic plants such as lilies and irises. The family Asteraceae is well represented, and is central to the region's spring flower displays. Grasses, unable to endure the seasonal stresses that shape the character of so many of the other plants, are scarce.

This semi-arid to arid zone has a varied and complex geology in which volcanic activity, and the accumulation of sand that washed down the Orange River over an immensely long period have played important roles. The physical appearance of the landscape, however, has largely been shaped by the fierce winds that pile sand up into the massive, regimented, 30-kilometre-long dunes of the Sperrgebiet and, elsewhere, clear the land of its sandy cover.

Wind erosion constantly exposes new surfaces to reveal a rich array of fossil deposits, especially in the Sperrgebiet, where sediment and rock have been weathered away to expose once-living forms as diverse as the springhare (*Parapedetes namaquensis*) and an ostrich-like diamond bird (*Diamantornis wardi*). One prospecting pit alone, at Arrisdrift, has yielded the fossils of fully eight mammalian orders, three orders of reptiles, and various birds and fishes – a testament to the biological diversity of a land that is now so hostile to living things.

Namaqualand is best known for its spectacular springtime blooms, their extent depending largely on the timing and amount of winter rain. The flowering season may last just a few weeks, from late July to September, though different areas are at their visual best at different times. On the Sandveld near the Atlantic coast, the flowers of the succulents tend to bloom for longer periods because they receive sustenance from the fog, and, unlike the plants of the interior, do not rely exclusively on the infrequent rains. The region's energy reserves are scarce and animals uncommon, so the wind disperses the seeds of most desert plants. The seeds are often shaped in such a way as to catch as much wind as possible, travelling many kilometres before settling. Others, though, do depend on insects for distribution, and it is thought that the variety and stridency of the floral colours are the product of competition for the attentions of the pollinators.

The plants of the region get their energy from the sun and their water from the rain or fog, but for its animals, finding food presents a perennial challenge: reserves are abundant for short periods, and life cycles are tied to the brief, favourable seasons. Many successful deserts animals – the scorpions and reptiles – can survive without eating for long periods. Defense mechanisms are also adaptive: many plants and animals are so coloured to blend with the environment; some, like the stone cricket, reveal themselves only when disturbed; others, such as the caddis fly larvae, build stony cases in which to hide from predators and the elements.

Lichens are dual organisms, comprising a symbiosis between fungi and algae – a combination which produces a living form unlike its constituent parts. Alone, neither component can survive: the fungal parts provide support and inorganic compounds; the algae, through photosynthesis, provide organic food.

Most of the succulent Karoo's plants and animals have adapted their behaviour, and physical structures to withstand the searing heat and the freezing cold, and to take advantage of the fog and rare rains. Many plants have fleshy leaves, or reflective bristles, and set seed quickly when conditions are ideal for germination. The region's few trees have also taken on unusual forms, many storing water in their fleshy trunks. The lives of many insects are also cued into the seasonal rainfall patterns of the region, the larvae and pupae of pollinating insects matching their diapause – the period of suspended development – with seed dormancy, so that the adults are ready to visit the plants when the latter are in full bloom.

THE DESERT'S UNIQUE FAUNA

Although the succulent Karoo has no endemic bird species, the region boasts three endemic mammals, all of them rodents – De Winton's golden mole (*Cryptochloris vintoni*), Van Zyl's golden mole (*C. zyli*) and the Namaqua dune mole rat (*Barhyergus janetta*). In addition, there is a rich reptilian fauna that thrives in the hot climate and which encompasses two snake species from the adder family (the desert mountain adder (*Bitis xeropaga*) and the Namaqua dwarf adder (*Bitis schneideri*)) and a great number of lizards, including five legless skinks, two species of burrowing skink and four girdled lizards. Surprisingly, the region also supports three kinds of endemic amphibians.

Most of the endemic species are burrowing animals, a behavioural pattern that not only allows them to survive in a hostile climate but may also contribute to the emdemicity, or distinctiveness, of the region, since burrowing tends to lead to geographic isolation.

Below *The Namaqua chameleon (**Chamaleo namaquensis**) uses its colour-changing abilities to turn black – so as to absorb heat in the cooler hours – or a pale shade of grey – so as to reflect heat when the sun is at its fiercest. To speed up the heating process, this chameleon stands with its body facing the sun, deflating its lungs and flattening its body to maximise its surface area for heat absorption.*

Below left **Crassula barklyi,** *one of the dwarf stone crop family, is found in the gravelly and shallow soils of the coastal areas. Like all succulents, it stores water in its fleshy leaves.*
Bottom left *These lichens at Alexander Bay depend on the fog rolling in from the Atlantic Ocean for their growth and survival. Lichens have the ability to extract moisture from the air, especially from the fog that sweeps across the land. Despite this, they are able to survive many years without water, and tend to grow very slowly. In most places in the world they cling to* rocks, *slowly eating away at the substrate, but on the less stabilised dunes of the succulent Karoo they flourish profusely on the sparse vegetation, or on the actual sand itself.*
Below right *The halfmens (**Pachypodium namaquanum**) derives its name from its likeness to human beings from afar. According to legend these trees were originally humans who came from the north, were separated from their tribe, and then turned into trees. Their 'heads' always turn to face the north, supposedly in desperate longing for the land from where they came.*

WEALTH BENEATH THE SANDS

The seeds of plants are not the only treasures hidden beneath the sands of the succulent Karoo. The seaboard is also rich in diamonds. Their discovery in 1908, near Lüderitz north of the Orange River mouth, was the beginning of a new era, one that would bring dramatic changes to the region.

The first prospecting rights were granted to a German company, and the ensuing boom prompted the establishment of a very busy little village called Kolmanskop, in close prox-

The Ever-present 'Mesems'

After flowering (1–3), some members of the *Mesembryanthemum* genus bear woody capsules (4) which enclose the plants' seeds. These capsules respond rapidly to rainfall, opening up (5 and 6) within minutes of the first drops. Some, indeed, need just a single raindrop for dispersal, releasing the tiny contents of their seed pods with the force of its impact.

There are about 2 500 species within the Mesembryanthemaceae family. Indeed it is the subcontinent's largest plant family, and the subject of endless taxonomic debates among scientists attempting to establish precise inter-relationships within the region's unique flora. Family members range from the tiny *Lithops*, or living stones, to the much larger dwarf shrubs.

Broadly speaking, though, mesems (known as 'vygies' in South Africa) are divided into two sub-families: the Mesembryanthemoideae, with nine genera, and the Ruschioidae with a staggering 107 genera. More than 90 per cent of the Ruschioidae's members are endemic to the succulent Karoo, which in biological terms makes it the richest of the world's semi-deserts.

imity to Lüderitz, being the site of the first find. Nowadays, Kolmanskop, at one time a beautiful town filled with splendour, is a ghost town, a poignant and sad place of old and derelict buildings and silent streets which are overlayed by the shifting desert sands. Then, in 1925, a casual prospector by the name of Jack Carstens picked up a diamond near Port Nolloth, south of the Orange River, and this area too began to yield its fabulous wealth (early in 1927 Hans Merensky and his team recovered no less than 12 500 carats in just six weeks). The coastal gravels were found to be richly diamondiferous from Kleinsee, south of Port Nolloth, northwards in

Right *Many desert succulents known as living stones or 'bokkloutjies' lie camouflaged, often only their colourful flowers betraying their presence in the stony ground.*

an 80-kilometre swathe to the Orange, and were also very well endowed around the fishing village of Alexander Bay.

In due course the Namaqualand diamond fields were declared State Alluvial Diggings, and for many decades the outside world was locked out. Over the past few years, however, the modern mine, currently being operated by Alexkor Limited, has allowed the public limited

access to visit and view the activities taking place, and even lays on tours of the mining areas. Unlike gold mining, digging for diamonds is essentially a surface activity that can inflict large and ugly scars on the environment. Powerful excavators must first remove vast amounts of sand (called overburden), under which lies the diamond-bearing gravel. Gravel deposits are located by means of modern prospecting techniques. Machines take the process further, breaking the earth and loading gravel onto trucks. As much as 95 tonnes of material has to be shifted in order to recover just one carat of diamond.

Over the years diamond mining has caused a lot of environmental damage. Old prospecting trenches and sterile mine blocks are a very common sight along the Namaqualand coast; overburden dumps and larger dumps at sorting plants, many of them hundreds of metres high, create surrealistic landscapes suggestive of a post-apocalyptic era within a coastal region of otherwise outstanding natural beauty. These relics of human activity are not only unsightly but can be harmful too: old, steep-walled mining blocks inhibit other land uses; strong winds blow sand off the mine dumps on to normally productive veld, smothering healthy vegetation and promoting that process which is turning fertile countryside into desert in so many other parts of Africa.

Ironically, though, diamond mining has had a positive effect on some areas in the past: it limited public access to the coastal regions.

Further, the mining areas are subject to surface operations, and those that have been spared the actual dynamite and bulldozers are among the best: the veld remains pristine and provides sanctuary for animals because it has not been subject to the erosive impact of domestic livestock farming. Elsewhere in the region, by contrast, the carrying capacity of the land for sheep and goats has decreased by more than half over the past 50 years. Goats will eat almost any plant and have taken their toll of the veld: the root systems that once protected the soils from the ravages of wind and rain can no longer bind the earth. Some areas are now totally useless for any form of farming, and are overgrown by inedible plants, notably those belonging to the genus *Euphorbia*.

Opposite *Members of the mongoose family, suricates (***Suricata suricatta***) are highly sociable and are common throughout the more arid regions of southern Africa. They are gregarious animals and live in extended family groups.*
Right *The bushman's candle (***Sarcocaulon patersonii***) is a deciduous plant, shedding its leaves each year to avoid excessive water loss during the drier months. Seen here is the plant as it appears before (***above***) and after (***below***) the rains. Many perennial desert plants have just a short period during the year's brief rains in which to grow flowers and set seed before returning to dormancy until the following year.*

The succulent Karoo was the scene of southern Africa's first game reserve. In 1892 the old Cape colonial government set aside an area of Bushmanland (named after its original inhabitants), but it enjoyed only a brief life: local farmers coveted the land for its agricultural potential and wiped out much of the wildlife, and the reserve was gradually de-proclaimed, divided and sold off. By 1920, less than 30 years after its inception, it had ceased to exist.

In recent years, however, a new sanctuary has made its welcome appearance. The Richtersveld National Park is located in the large bend of the Orange River, and is being developed into a prime ecotourism destination by the National Parks Board in association with local communities. The task is not without its difficulties: the area is isolated, its climate inhospitable, and it is suitable only for low-impact tourism – which is something of a problem since visitors are most attracted to the place during certain, brief, periods of the year, notably the wild-flower season.

Other development projects are being investigated so as to determine the actual viability of irrigation schemes along the Orange River, but this once-great watercourse is now virtually a ghost of its former self: irrigation upriver is taxing its flow to the point where the ecologically valuable estuary may already be doomed. It is entirely possible that, by the end of this century, water will only occasionally reach the river mouth, and much of the plant and animal life of the region will have suffered irreparable damage by that time.

Left *The succulent Karoo is a forbidding environment, where the struggle for life continues on its fragile soils at a pace that is difficult for the casual observer to appreciate. Damage to such a delicate ecosystem, like other arid ecosystems, will take a long time to recover and the tracks of modern humans may lie here forever.*

Below left *An abandoned building in one of southern Namibia's ghost towns has been preserved by the dry desert air, an eerie reminder of the region's more prosperous days when diamonds drew prospectors to the bounty of the succulent Karoo.*

Below *The stone cricket is cryptically shaped and coloured to look like a rock. This species' camouflage is a vital defence against its predators such as lizards, snakes and birds. When seriously threatened, this insect can leap to safety using its powerful hind legs.*

Bottom *Throughout vast areas of Namaqualand goats are now the only animals which can be sustained by the land because they will eat almost any available plant.*

The Marine Realm

THE TWO OCEANS

Beyond Africa's southern coasts lies a marine world so vast and diverse it defies most

earthly comparisons. Like so many terrestrial environments,

though, it too is under serious threat.

Between Cape Point and Cape Agulhas two of the earth's great oceans, the Atlantic and the Indian, merge together. The first European sailors to navigate the meeting of the two oceans off Africa's most southerly point named it L'Agulhas, 'the needle', for they found that only here were their compasses not affected by magnetic deviation but bore 'directly upon the true poles of the earth'. Cape Agulhas has since given its name to one of the world's most powerful ocean currents, the Agulhas Current. At more than 160 kilometres wide and spanning more than 2 000 kilometres of coastline, this ocean current delivers more than 80 million tons of warm water to the south and east coast of southern Africa.

To the west there is another great ocean stream – the Benguela Current, which flows northwards. The cold waters of this current are rich in oxygen, nitrates and phosphates, and in plankton which support an abundance of primary feeders – in turn providing food for large numbers of fish.

Ocean currents, their temperatures in particular, determine the nature and the migratory patterns of much of the marine life, including those of the large vertebrates – descendants of terrestrial species that, aeons ago, left the land to return to the oceans.

Above *The vast open oceans support immense shoals of fish. The geelbek (**Atractoscion aequidens**), featured here, is one such species. When sexually mature, this fish migrates with the sardine run in winter from Cape waters through to KwaZulu-Natal.*
Left *The plough snail (**Bullia digitalis**) can reach an age of up to 20 years, which means that it grows very slowly. Much of this animal's life is spent passively beneath the sand in an effort to conserve energy; it emerges only when food is scented.*
Right *The powerful force of the ocean beats relentlessly against the coast of southern Africa. More than just an inspiring sight, these coastal waters support a startling diversity of marine life.*

MAMMALS AND REPTILES
OF THE OCEAN

Among the larger creatures of the ocean are the Cetaceans, a mammal group that comprises dolphins and whales, and of which various kinds can be seen off the southern seaboard. However, despite their emancipation from the land and their ability to remain underwater for long periods, these animals have lungs rather than gills and must come to the surface regularly to take in air.

The dolphins, commonly seen cruising the offshore surf in search of prey, are among the most intelligent of all mammals, often living in close-knit, interdependent social groups. They have poor eyesight, but more than make up for the deficiency with an in-built radar system called echolocation – sound waves, usually highly pitched squeaks, clicks and whistles, are emitted which, when reflected back, give

information about the size, shape, location and even density of the object encountered. On occasions these emissions are loud enough to disorientate and stun the prey.

Their Cetacean cousins, the whales, are also frequent visitors to the southern African coast. For most of the year they plough the productive southern ocean in search of plankton, krill and other small crustaceans which comprise most of their diet. At the beginning of this century these giant mammals were hunted almost to extinction for their blubber, but their numbers have recovered somewhat in recent times. The southern right whale (*Balaena glacialis*) is now the commonest of the whales seen off the coast, the adult females seeking its sheltered bays between June and December each year to give birth to and nurse their young – which, like all mammals, are reared on a diet of mother's milk until they are able to fend for themselves (a calf can consume as much as

400 litres of milk a day). The southern right population of these seas declined by more than 90 per cent after large-scale whaling began in the 19th century, but an international ban on hunting and the establishment of a whale sanctuary in the southern ocean have stabilised their numbers. Other species such as fin (*Balaenoptera physalus*), sei (*Balaenoptera borealis*) and minke (*Balaenoptera acutorostrata*) whales are smaller and less numerous visitors, but also breed in these coastal waters. Their numbers, too, are on the increase.

Among other prominent marine mammals are the seals, which breed communally, favouring predator-free offshore islands to give birth (only the Cetaceans, which were earlier terrestrial invaders of the oceans, have evolved seagoing reproduction). Many of the pups fall prey to the fierce southeasterly gales, others to the ocean's predators – notably sharks, among which the great white (*Carcharodon*

Opposite *The jackass penguin (**Spheniscus demersus**) is South Africa's only penguin species. Like many other sea birds, courtship between mates and pair bonding activity such as preening are well developed and fulfil important functions in these birds' lives.*

Top *Dolphins, including the dusky dolphin (**Lagenorhynchus obscurus**) illustrated here, are among the most intelligent of all mammals, often living in close-knit, interdependent social groups. Since dolphins have poor eyesight, they rely on an in-built radar system to find their way.*

Above, left *More than a 100 shark species occur along the southern African coast. Some, like the ragged-tooth shark (**Carcharias taurus**), are regularly encountered by scuba divers.*
Above, right *The southern right whale rises upside down to the surface to feed on plankton.*

carcharias) is perhaps the most fearsome and efficient. Seals, and particularly their pups, form a large part of the six-metre monster's diet despite its preference for the deeper off-shore waters. Attacks on humans have also been recorded, most often around the coastal islands where seals breed.

Then there are the turtles, ancient marine animals that have travelled the earth's great oceans since the dinosaurs ruled the world. Like all reptiles, turtles are cold-blooded creatures which depend on their surroundings for warmth, so southern Africa's species are confined to the ocean waters of the Agulhas Current. The region is home to five of these and, like many terrestrial vertebrates which have adapted to a marine life – and despite their long evolutionary span in the oceans – they must return to land in order to reproduce. Some in fact travel as far as 3 000 kilometres from their feeding grounds to reach the pre-ordained nesting sites, unerringly homing in on that exact patch of sand in which they themselves were born, perhaps as long as 40 and more years before. After mating, the females drag themselves ashore on their ungainly flippers to dig a deep hole, and to lay their eggs, in the soft sands.

Top *The sandy shores of the southern African coast may appear barren and lifeless on the surface, yet within the sands life exists in abundance on a microscopic scale.*

Above *The pink ghost crab (**Ocypode ryderi**) is an inhabitant of the east coast where, like* **Tylos** *species on the west coast, it digs burrows in the sand around the high tide mark. This crab is predatory and may feed on turtle hatchlings as they struggle to reach the sea.*

Right *A female leatherback turtle (**Dermochelys coriacea**) may produce as many as 1 000 eggs per season in batches of one to two hundred. Despite this prodigious effort by the female, it is likely that for every nesting female only one off-spring will survive to reproduce itself one day.*

Tylos, *the Giant Isopod*

Along the beaches of the west coast, the giant isopod Tylos granulatus *often emerges from its sandy burrow near the high-tide mark to feed on washed-up kelp and other ocean debris. This creature times its feeding activity to coincide with night-time low tides, and is most commonly seen during neap tides. Like all isopods, including woodlice, its terrestrial relatives, it can roll into a tight ball when alarmed; a tough-plated carapace affords it protection against its natural enemies. Only when it senses that it is out of danger will it crawl back to the high-tide mark where once again it digs itself into the moist sand. Increasing use of off-road vehicles along the west coast beaches appears to be causing a decline in the numbers of these creatures.*

THE SANDY SHORES

Some of the most attractive parts of the southern coast are its sandy beaches, which account for more than 40 per cent of the shoreline.

Below *Barnacles (***Tetraclita serrata** *on the left and* **Octomeris angulosa** *on the right) use their rear appendages to filter food from the sea. These animals start out in life as planktonic larvae. When they are ready to settle, the larvae metamorphose into adults and glue their heads to a rock surface, choosing rocks exposed during low tide and thereby preventing desiccation.*

The sandy shores may seem bare, but appearances are deceptive: here there is life, though most of it exists on a scale that is too small for the naked eye to see. Plants, of course, are unable to establish themselves on the shifting surface, but some highly specialised animals do exist in this unlikely environment, many surviving as suspension feeders, living on what the tide brings in and escaping the onslaught of the ocean rollers by burrowing beneath the surface. Among them is the white mussel of the genus *Donax*, which has a fleshy foot that it uses to dig itself in; it feeds on small particles carried in by the waves, circulating the water with its two projecting siphons.

One of the more curious of the beach animals is the plough snail (*Bullia digitalis*), a shelled mollusc which feeds on dead and decaying material that is washed up. It will eat pretty well anything organic, though red bait, rotting fish and the blue-bottle (*Physalia physalis*) are its favoured foods. Natural selection has devised a most ingenious method of locomotion for the plough snail in its bid to maintain its position ahead of the tide: it spends most of its time sitting below the sand with only its siphon protruding, testing the water above much like the sand mussel. But when the tide recedes it emerges and spreads its foot wide against the water current and surfs down the beach, heading for the spot where its food is most likely to be deposited. These molluscs have an uncanny sense of smell: the very barest of chemical signal enables them to locate a potential meal. After gorging themselves with as much as a third of their own body weight, plough snails bury themselves once more, remaining hidden until the tide falls.

THE ROCKY SHORES

The sandy coastal expanses are punctuated by rocky outcrops which support a mosaic of plant and animal life – an ecosystem entirely dependent on the intertidal substrate. The living areas of the various organisms are organised vertically – that is, they are geared to the conditions prevailing at the different tidal levels, and at each level there is a delicate balance between the forces of dehydration, wave action and immersion: a balance that produces' some of nature's most fascinating structural and behavioural adaptations.

Seaweeds mantle much of the rock towards the lower reaches of the intertidal zone, forming a rich botanical garden that provides shelter from the waves both for animals and algal plants, though they have to compete for space on which to grow and feed. Here, attachment to the rock is all important, and algal plants tend to be fewer where the waves are strong. The nutritious algal surface sustains a variety of grazing animals, among which shelled

Right *The limpet* **Patella longicosta** *(top left corner) aggressively guards its territory from potential intruders by using its shell to lift up and push away other limpets.*

Below *Space for growth, feeding and photosynthesis is often limited on rocky shores and many limpet species,* **Patella argenvillei**, *for example, may spend much of their life waiting patiently for the day when a nearby death vacates a larger territory.*

Left *Much of the southern African west coast is dominated by thick beds of kelp and sea-bamboo that extend far offshore. They provide an important source of food and nutrients for many animals, and their thick growth offers shelter from the force of the waves.*
Above and right *The limpet* Patella argenvillei's *feeding strategy involves raising its shell and trapping algae, and particularly kelp that may pass beneath it.*

molluscs are prominent. Most recognisable among the countless inhabitants of intertidal shores are the limpets, many of which clamp themselves tightly to the rock surface, forming 'home-scars' to which they will return after every grazing foray in search of the tiny settling algal spores on which they feed. They scrape these spores from the rock with a rasping organ known as a radula.

Coastal waters are usually richer in nutrients than is the open ocean, and many animals – barnacles, mussels, anemones and fan worms among them – employ a whole range of structural adaptations to filter food in suspension.

Similar dynamics govern the intertidal zones of the West Coast, where there isn't so wide a diversity of species; the total biomass of species here is significantly higher than that of organisms along the southern and eastern shorelines, however. These western waters are among the world's most productive because the upwelling of the ocean brings huge quantities of nutrients to the surface where they are incorporated into the food chain. A proliferation of algal growth, forming underwater forests of kelp and sea-bamboo, supports a wide array of species ranging from limpets and fish to seabirds and seals.

SUBTIDAL LIFE

Below the intertidal zone, in a rocky world that is always submerged, life flourishes in even greater abundance, the undersea gardens embracing a quite remarkable profusion of

Left *The black oystercatcher (**Haematopus moquini**) feeds on shellfish, playing a vital role in controlling the numbers of these herbivores. However, as a result of human activity it is now among the coast's most endangered species.*
Below *Mankind's desire to gaze across a vast ocean and play in its waves is putting more and more pressure on a coastline that is fast running out of natural wilderness.*

shapes, sizes and colours and, in one of southern Africa's largest marine reserves, off the Tsitsikamma coast, a series of spectacular underwater reefs.

In deeper waters, though, less light manages to penetrate and the algal life, so prolific on the rocky shores, is unable to survive. Dominating this murky environment are primitive animals that take on an array of plant-like forms – sponges, sea-squirts, sea-fans, anemones and

corals, including many species that have yet to be scientifically described. These animals support shellfish such as crabs and crayfish; higher up the food chain are various kinds of reef fish – including white musselcracker (*Sparodon durbanensis*), roman (*Chrysoblephus laticeps*), red stumpnose (*Chrysoblephus gibbiceps*) and galjoen (*Coracinus capensis*). Unlike the fish of the open ocean, many of these reef species lead solitary lives, establishing independent

territories and living to a great age. The shallow waters of the continental shelf are often disturbed by coastal storms that recirculate the nutrients, and many of the species – notably the soft corals – are adapted to filter feeding, capturing the 'rain' of nutrients that drift by.

THE OPEN OCEAN

Although the southern waters are warmed by the Agulhas Current, the ocean here is surprisingly low in nutrients. But as the Agulhas meets the colder South Atlantic Current, productive fronts develop, the interface stimulating the growth of phytoplankton. These microscopic plants form the basis of most of the ocean's food chain, account for more than half of the world's photosynthetic activity and cycle much of the world's oxygen and carbon dioxide through their cells. As they drift close to the surface, they are preyed upon by microscopic animals known as zooplankton – minute crustaceans related to crabs and lobsters.

Cuttlefish and squid are experts at underwater locomotion, and are joined by fish such as elf (*Pomatomus saltatrix*) and giant yellowtail (*Seriola lalandi*) to hunt the smaller fish species – anchovy (*Engraulis japonicus*) and pilchard (*Sardinops sagax*), for example – which congregate in their millions to feed on the food-rich surface layers of zooplankton. These surface waters are warm and provide ideal conditions for even larger predatory fish. Other species seek the safety of the deeper, colder waters, some – such as squid – descending to the ocean floor to breed and lay their eggs. But this environment also has its specialist predators, which feed and hunt individually rather than in the great schools of the open ocean above.

Many pelagic (living near the surface) fish migrate to find favourable conditions – those suitable for breeding and those offering food, which tends to be more abundant in frontal areas where currents interact. Other species have no particular migratory route but will simply follow the warm waters of the Agulhas Current. Among them are Skipjack tuna (*Katsuwonus pelamis*), yellowtail and Cape snoek (*Thyrsites atun*), streamlined predators specially adapted for speed and known as the 'cheetahs of the ocean'.

THE HUMAN ASSAULT

Man's association with the coastal environment goes back as far as 150 000 years, to a time when hunter-gatherer societies first harvested their protein-rich resources. Many of the seaboard's caves have yielded evidence of prehistoric habitation, their great middens of shells and bones representing a wide variety of sea creatures. These resources, until recent times, were eminently sustainable.

But then came the colonial settlers, and exploitation on a massive scale so that today the ocean larder is approaching exhaustion.

In less than 200 years the whales were hunted to the brink of extinction. Advances in technology, including sophisticated nets and trawling techniques, led to the collapse of the harvests; in the sixties, the massive pilchard stocks crashed, shattering an industry that supported entire communities of people. The off-shore angling industry also took its toll: less than 50 years ago coastal anglers boasted record hauls of reef fish; nowadays, catches are 75 per cent less than when records began. But despite these alarming figures, more than two and a half million tons of fish are still caught each year.

The modern world also continues the assault in other ways. Coastal mining despoils long stretches of coastline. Elsewhere, it is the very beauty of this coastal environment that is its greatest threat as residential and recreational development proliferates. Along the coasts of the former Ciskei and Transkei regions, hungry villagers strip the shores of all that may be eaten. Elsewhere, even protected reserves pose no deterrent to poachers who disregard catch limits and sell expensive seafood to an ever more popular restaurant trade.

Yet it is still possible for human society to live in harmony with this rich environment. More marine reserves must be set aside; fishing controls have to be tightened and more efficiently monitored. The great hope for the future, though, lies in the very vastness of the oceans. They cover more than two-thirds of our earth, and marine ecosystems, unlike terrestrial food chains, are much larger and less vulnerable to disruption. But if we do succeed in wrecking these ecosystems, as we have so many on the land, the future of our planet will be at risk.

The Grazing Lands

THE BUSHVELD AND SAVANNA

The sunlit savanna and bushveld areas of southern Africa

are without parallel in the abundance

and variety of their mammals, both large and small.

When one thinks of game sanctuaries, the great African savannas spring to mind, bringing images of vast buffalo herds, of lordly giraffe, of vast concourses of wildebeest and zebra and antelope grazing peacefully on the endless plains, and of the hunt and kill, the everrecurring drama in which the primordial rituals of the wilderness are played out. Savanna, in the African context, generally refers to open ground covered in tall grasses and shrubs. Trees are irregular, but in the thicker bushveld regions they form a loose tangle of vegetation among rocky outcrops.

Stretching in a broad fringe along the east side of Africa, through the Great Rift Valley as far as South Africa, the savanna supports an extraordinary diversity of mammal species. It is at its most splendid, perhaps, in the bigger southern and eastern reserves, most especially in Kenya's famed Serengeti, a name which literally means 'endless place' and whose sweet grasslands

sustain two million wildebeest, half a million antelope, a quarter of a million zebra. In turn, these animals support more than 2 000 lion and 700 cheetah, as well as hyaena and leopard. To the south, reserves are not so large but Zambia's Luangwa Valley, Zimbabwe's Hwange and South Africa's renowned Kruger National Park preserve similar ecosystems, although only in the Serengeti do the herds migrate as they have done, spectacularly, since time immemorial.

Above *A small herd of impala (***Aepyceros melampus***) cautiously drinks from a bushveld waterhole. During the dry season most animals require surface water and do not stray too far from a ready source..*
Left *The whitebacked vulture (***Gyps africanus***), spread throughout southern Africa, is often seen soaring above the plains in search of carrion.*
Right *Resting with its kill in the safety of a tree, a leopard (***Panthera pardus***) sleeps through the day until the dark of night, when this nocturnal predator stirs into action again.*

THE FERTILE PLAINS

The climate throughout much of the savanna regions is characterised by irregular periods of rain alternating with long dry spells – conditions which, combined with regular veld-burning (either spontaneous or deliberate), favour the growth of expansive grasslands. Here and there umbrella-like acacia thorn trees and bushes dot the landscape, mostly near the banks of rivers, lakes and dry watercourses. Acacias are the predominant but not the only species: there are other distinctive trees, among them the giant and ancient baobabs, which store water in their broad, fleshy trunks. However, the bulk of the savanna's plant life comprises grasses, many of which have specialised, widely branching under-ground creepers called rhizomes. Unlike other plants, grasses grow from a point that is protected beneath the soil, and so they are able to recover quickly after their upper parts have been grazed by herbivores, or scorched by fire.

When rains are good the savanna grasslands become rich enough to support as many as 150 animals on each acre. The herbivores consume huge quantities of food, and the net energy loss from the savanna ecosystem would be unsustainable were it not returned in some way, much of it through the digestive systems of animals themselves. Great quantities of dung are deposited to fertilise the soil – trodden to dust, which either soaks in with the rains or is parcelled up into little balls by dung-beetles (belonging to the Scarabidae family) that follow the scent of the fresh droppings.

But the vast majority of insects feed on the vegetation in a more direct manner: beetles, bugs and caterpillars often living in close association with a particular plant (known as a host-plant). In some cases the insect depends on its host simply for food and shelter; in others the relationship has evolved further, to the mutual benefit of host and guest – by way of pollination in the case of butterflies and moths, or as a protective arrangement. Acacias, for example, provide an exellent source of food for the biting ants, which return the favour by deterring browsing animals from eating their leaves. Mammals also have working relationships with acacias, especially when it comes to seed dispersal: many kinds of seeds will fail to germinate unless they have first passed through the gut of a herbivore.

THE BUSHVELD

Not all of the savanna comprises grassland. Where water is more abundant, or where fires have failed to make an impact, grasses give way to thick bush and to trees. Here, as the habitat becomes more varied, the simple grass-herbivore-predator food chain of the plains is superseded by more complex relationships. Rocky outcrops, river banks and broken bush provide new niches for a host of other mammal species and an array of birds and reptiles.

Among the larger reptiles are the snakes, biggest of which is the African python (*Python sebae*), which can grow to six metres in length and can capture, kill and eat a small antelope. Pythons overcome their prey with thick, muscular constricting coils: as each breath of the victim is exhaled, so the coils squeeze a little tighter until the animal finally suffocates. Venomous snakes capture their prey in a very different way, some injecting the neurotoxins from two sharp teeth, or fangs, into the bloodstream of their victim – a technique especially effective against mammals because of their fast circulatory system. The venom of some snakes works in two ways: it immobilises and quickly

Opposite *Southern Africa's top predator, the lion (***Panthera leo***), feasts on a freshly killed warthog (***Phacochoerus aethiopicus***).*
Right *The African elephant (***Loxodonta africana***), the world's largest terrestrial animal, uses trumpeting calls to indicate alarm.*
Below *Termite mounds play a critical role in the veld ecology throughout many biomes. These primitive insects have remained largely unchanged for more than 200 million years.*

overcomes the victim and then, because of the enzymes it contains, initiates the digestive process before the animal is even swallowed. Such meals take less time to digest, and the snake is active again soon after eating. Vipers, mambas and cobras all feed in this way.

THE HERBIVORES

Africa's grassland and savanna regions support an astonishing variety of herbivorous mammals – antelope for the most part, but also rhinoceros, elephant, zebra, giraffe and others. Elephants rank as the largest and also some of the longest-living of the land mammals, some surviving to 50 years and more. They are mixed feeders, able to eat a wide range of plant material including grasses, leaves and bark. They are even known to push down whole trees to get at the tender shoots at the top. For them, a catholic diet is essential because each day a single adult must consume up to 300 kilograms of food and spend up to 16 hours foraging. Thus, large herds can have a profound effect on the bushveld, especially if they are restricted, unable to roam freely over a wide range. When unrestricted, though, their feeding patterns maintain open grassland and keep the bush and forest from encroaching on the savanna. And although their habits appear destructive, they play an important ecological role, rarely killing a tree but, rather, shaping it and keeping its growth low. The elephant, which is considered one of the most intelligent of all animals, lives in close-knit groups dominated by females. Bulls are often found alone or in small bachelor groups, but join the females for breeding purposes.

Below *Baobabs* (**Adansonia digitata**) *are the largest and oldest of southern African trees.* **Right** *The warthog inhabits open grassland, often near water, but avoids areas of thick bush.* **Opposite** *A white rhinoceros* (**Ceratotherium simum**) *calf takes a break from grazing the short grasses of the veld. These pachyderms have wide, flat mouths which enable them to crop the grasses to almost ground level.*

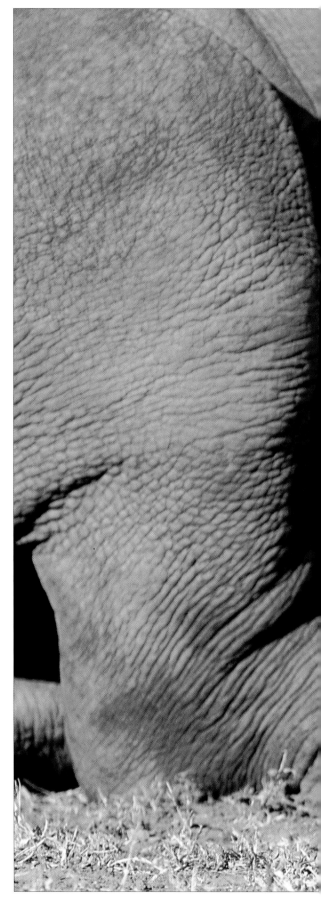

Above *The giraffe (**Giraffa camelopardalis**) has adapted to feeding on leaves of tall trees by way of a long neck and tongue, and prehensile lips.*
Left *The mopane worm is actually a caterpillar that lives and feeds in close association with the mopane tree.*
Opposite *The stripes of the Burchell's zebra (**Equus burchellii**) are a form of camouflage, making them less visible to predators.*

The rhinoceros, second largest of the land mammals, ranged throughout the African continent, Asia and Europe until the last ice age. There are two African species, both with poor eyesight but endowed with acute hearing and a keen sense of smell. The white, or square-lipped, rhinoceros (*Ceratotherium simum*) grazes the open savanna, where it crops the grasses with broad muscular lips. The slightly

smaller and rarer black rhinoceros (*Diceros bicornis*) browses on low bush with more dextrous, prehensile lips that are able to reach among the thorns to the leafy shoots. Both rhinoceros and elephant are oblivious to the thorns of many acacias, and without their browsing attention these trees and bushes would proliferate out of control. Giraffes (*Giraffa camelopardalis*) are the tallest of the mammals, able to feed on the highest acacia branches, and are found along the edges of the plains where trees are more abundant.

TALL AS THE TREES

The giraffe is an evolutionary object-lesson, superbly adapted to its food source. Apart from a long neck and prehensile lips, it has a long tongue that enables it to negotiate thorns in order to grasp bunches of leaves, and a specialised heart and valve system that pumps blood up the extended neck to the head. Without this valve system the animal would have a problem in accessing water: the head must first be lowered, which without the valves would bring a lethal rush of blood to the brain, but the valves of the neck compensate by reducing the pressure. In order to reach the water, too, the animal has to lower itself on splayed legs – an ungainly drinking position that puts it at particular risk from predators during its visits to waterholes.

Because of the widely differing feeding strategies of the savanna's antelope and other animals, the veld is able to sustain a great diversity of the larger species. Zebras, for example, prefer to graze on the tall, fibrous grasses among which their vertical stripes provide ideal camouflage. Sharp incisor teeth cut the grass, which is then pulped by large molars and passes through a long digestive system that contains a mass of bacteria. The bacteria ferment the grass in the stomach and the products of the process, as well as the bacteria themselves, are then absorbed by the animal. As the zebras crop the veld, so other species of grass proliferate, opening up new feeding opportunities for a variety of antelope species. In contrast to antelope, which are ruminants (food is regurgitated from the stomach and chewed once more), zebras have a relatively inefficient digestive system and need to consume much more than their fellow herbivores to make up for the lower nutritional value extracted from their diet.

A classic savanna scene encompasses black wildebeest (*Connochaetes gnou*), Burchell's zebra (*Equus burchellii*) and impala (*Aepyceros melampus*) grazing together across the plains, while among them red hartebeest (*Alcephalus*

Above *The lithe cheetah (***Acinonyx jubatus***) stretches before a day's hunting. These cats specialise in catching small antelope.*

buselaphus) find nourishment in the tougher, drier stalks which many other species ignore. Each animal has a slightly different functional relationship with the veld, and in this way the impact of the grazing multitudes is distributed over a wide range of vegetation types.

Antelope might appear placid while grazing, but can turn highly aggressive within their own social structures, especially in the mating season. During the rut, male wildebeest can often be seen challenging one another, snorting and stamping around in an effort to establish a territory, and so attract a mate. Ritualised aggression sometimes fails to resolve a conflict and is replaced by charges and head-butting, for which horns have become adapted. Each antelope species has its own growth form of tough horn, ranging from the majestic spiral of the kudu to the lyre-shaped curves of the hartebeest. These horns also have defensive value against predators, most especially those of the gemsbok (*Oryx gazella*), groups of which have been known to lower their heads menacingly to see off a pride of threatening lion.

THE CARNIVORES

Just as the herbivores are adapted to feed in different ways, so each carnivore has developed its own special ways of hunting. Bringing down a large antelope while on the run is by no means a simple task, and in the midst of a stampeding herd can be downright dangerous. Largest and most spectacular of the carnivores are the lions, which prey on some of the savanna's biggest animals – zebra, buffalo, young giraffe and even rhinoceros are all known to number among their victims. Lions are among the best organised predators, hunting cooperatively in prides of extended family groups that include females, adolescent males and cubs.

Just as impressive in their own fashion are the other big cats. Cheetahs, which usually target small antelope, lack the robust physique of the lion, but can travel at phenomenal speed over short distances. The leopard, the caracal and the genet are more active at night, hunting by stealth and ambush.

Not all the carnivores belong to the cat family, however. There is good evidence that the spotted hyaena (*Crocuta crocuta*), despite its reputation, is a highly successful hunter, actually catching more prey than it scavenges. These animals also hunt in packs, which are often large enough to chase lions away from the kill. The brown hyaena (*Hyaena brunnea*), by contrast, is a solitary hunter and scavenger.

The most efficient and highly cooperative of African pack hunters are the wild dogs (*Lycaon pictus*), which have adapted to operate over huge ranges. Running in groups of up to 40 individuals, they will tirelessly pursue prey as large as zebra until the victim finally falters. Exhausted, the prey animal is attacked from every angle and is quickly brought down.

The disposal of a carcass follows an unchanging pattern. After the successful hunters have had their fill and retire to digest their meal, jackals snatch scraps, hyaenas use their powerful jaws to crush the bones and flocks of vultures join the melee to scavenge whatever they can. Invariably, several vulture species are involved. So efficient is the process that, within a few hours, the only remaining evidence of the kill is a few large bones and a smear of blood on the veld.

THE LAST REFUGE

For many centuries, pastoral African societies herded their cattle over the great sunlit spaces without serious threat to the environment: their numbers were relatively few, the veld was seemingly limitless and, in any case, nagana (a sleeping sickness brought by the tsetse fly) and other sicknesses restricted the range of the domestic herds, maintaining some sort of a balance between man and the wilderness.

Then the European settlers arrived with farming skills, their guns and their passion for the killing sport. Nineteenth-century Africa was a mecca for the Victorian hunter-adventurer, and wild game was slaughtered in its millions. To make matters worse, the new breeds of cattle, introduced by the settlers, brought new

diseases: outbreaks of rinderpest devastated the herbivore populations. And many more were culled in well-meaning but tragically misguided attempts to eradicate the tsetse fly.

Over the decades the relentless expansion of the farmlands, and an exploding population, its mining operations, its roads, railways, power lines and fences have battered Africa's most extensive biome almost beyond recognition, reducing it to a scatter of parks and reserves. In only a few places can one now witness the great migrations of the herds, and the gene pools of many species have shrunk to near-critical levels. Poaching is rampant.

But there is hope. Environmental concern is now fashionable, and pressure on decision-makers is mounting. More significant, perhaps, is the lure of profit: the benefits of ecotourism are now widely recognised, and more and more land is being set aside for conservation. The large-scale movement of game, though – a critical component of the savanna's natural cycle – is no longer possible, so to maintain the artificially created ecosystem and the carrying capacity of the parks, the numbers have to be controlled. In Zimbabwe, Botswana and north-eastern South Africa the elephant populations are so well protected that the herds have grown too large for the environment and have to be culled.

The surplus animals of other flourishing mammal species enjoy a kinder fate: they are translocated to sanctuaries elsewhere. Perhaps, though, a longer-lasting and general-

ly far more satisfactory solution would be to develop corridors between reserves, even across political borders, to create a more natural system, one with greater diversity.

Ironically, as the mineral wealth of the subcontinent becomes exhausted, game parks and reserves may come to represent a country's biggest foreign currency earner. That impetus, if properly handled, can only benefit what remains of the savanna wilderness.

Below left *The consuming of a kill takes on a typical succession involving various animals: after the predator responsible has had its fill, scavengers, such as vultures and marabou storks* (**Leptoptilos crumeniferus**), *take over.*
Below right *Most herbivores share the predator defence strategy of herding which provides a safe environment in which to rear young.*
Right *A safari in a protected reserve is now the only available way to appreciate the bushveld.*

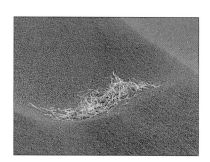

The Desert Lands

THE NAMIB AND KALAHARI

Flying high above the desert landscape, one's first impression is of utter desolation –

fierce, forbidding, often featureless environments lacking any sign of human activity. Yet the desert

sustains a surprising variety of unusual, often unique, life forms.

Throughout the Namib Desert tier upon parallel tier of massive, red-brown, barren-looking dunes stretch to the far horizons, up the seaboard towards the Kuiseb River. Over the long months of drought the dunes inch their way northwards to invade the bone-dry riverbed itself, only to be washed away during those rare occasions when the water does come down in flood. This is the southern section of the Namib, the world's most ancient and arguably most fascinating desert. North of the Kuiseb the seemingly endless sands give way to gravel plains which are so smooth they appear to have been swept by a giant broom, the huge monotony relieved by the occasional outcrop that stands like an island in the grey-green ocean of gravel. It seems that nothing can grow, nothing can live in this arid, alien, sun-blasted land. Only after a careful look can one detect life such as lichens among the rocks. And there are other, more complex life forms hidden in the desert depths; plants and animals that survive by virtue of special, and sometimes surprising, adaptations that enable them to conserve water and withstand intense heat.

DESERT PARAMETERS

In broad terms a desert can be said to be an area where the evaporation rate of water is far greater than the average rainfall, and in the central Namib mean precipitation has been measured at just 18 millimetres –

Above *Windblown detritus (grasses and seeds) accumulates in dune hollows and forms the basis of the Namib Desert's dune food chain.*
Left *The dwarf beaked snake (**Dipsina multimaculata**) hides in loose sand.*
Right *South of Walvis Bay the red sands of the Namib Desert meet the cold waters of the Atlantic Ocean. This interaction produces coastal fog banks that provide essential moisture for desert life.*

200 times less than the evaporation rate. The little rain that does fall is unpredictable and highly localised, often occurring in flash-flood downpours. There is little ground cover, in the form of plants or physical features, and little shelter so essential for the survival of wildlife.

The Namib is the harshest of southern Africa's desert regions, stretching in a band 100 to 150 kilometres wide along the coastal region of southwestern Namibia. Exactly where its northern and southern borders lie depends on what definition of a desert one accepts: some argue that the Namib starts at the Olifants

Left *The spectacular desert elephant roams through Kaokoland.*
Below left *The wedge-snouted desert lizard* (**Meroles cuneirostris**) *lives in the red dunes of the Namib. It combats the heat by performing a 'thermoregulatory dance', lifting each foot in turn off the hot sand. When the heat of the sand gets too much to endure, it dives into the cooler layers of sand.*
Below right *The sidewinding adder* (**Bitis peringueyi**) *swallows its prey whole.*

River in South Africa and extends as far north as southern Angola; others that its southern limit is in the Lüderitz area, north of the Orange River mouth. From a practical point of view, though, the issue is largely academic: the reality is that, from the Olifants River northwards, the land becomes progressively more arid, and the driest and least vegetated part lies along the Namibian coast.

MOISTURE IN A DRY LAND

Like the seaboard of the succulent Karoo to the south, life in the Namib would be impossible without the coastal fog that periodically rolls in from the cold Atlantic Ocean. Fog is typical along the southwestern African coasts, though here it tends to last for much longer periods. Some areas may be fog-bound for as many as 180 days a year. As the mists spread eastwards over the sands they dissipate in the heat of the sun. At their furthest extent they carry precious moisture 70 kilometres inland.

Since rainfall is so rare in the Namib, many species have evolved special features that enable them to collect moisture from the

atmosphere. Among them are the lichens already mentioned, of which there are numerous varieties – indeed they are among the world's most widespread organisms, and are prolific along the coastal belt of the Namib. These simple living forms, which have intricate textures and a range of soft colours, encrust the rocks and even the quartz pebbles of the gravel plains. They are very slow-growing, and in dry periods they fold up their leaf-like thalluses to reduce water loss and expose their silvery lower surfaces to reflect heat. When rain falls or the dew is heavy, the thalluses quickly unfold to reveal their photosynthetic side.

In fact, the Namib, despite appearances, has a wealth of strange and fascinating plants ranging from the remarkable *Welwitschia mirabilis* to low-growing cryptic succulents of the genera *Lithops* and *Fenestraria*, many of which play prominent roles in the desert ecology.

The !Nara plant (*Acanthosicyos horridus*), for example, is a wild cucurbit that grows in the dunes; it has deep, water-searching roots, and serves as an important dune stabiliser, helping to solidify and compact the substrate by trapping sand swept in by the wind. Moreover,

condensed fog from its leaves drips to the ground to provide a habitat for many small creatures and the compacted soil becomes solid enough to accommodate burrows. The plant also provides food and shade for many non-burrowing life forms.

Generally, the leaves of the desert plants are much reduced (and sometimes, indeed, nonexistent): broad, thin leaves are a luxury only afforded in wetter climates, where rapid water loss can easily be recovered by root uptake. The !Nara is among the species that have no true leaves: photosynthesis takes place in stems and spines that contain green chlorophyll.

The Namib's habitats range from the gravel plains, rocky outcrops and red dune seas to the seasonal river courses that run westwards across the desert, though few ever reach the sea. These rivers act as life-giving corridors for plant species, enabling them to extend their distribution far into the desert itself, and their beds sustain scatters of large, mostly acacia thorn trees. Two species, the anaboom (*Acacia albida*) and the camelthorn (*Acacia erioloba*), thrive along the course of the Kuiseb and, in turn, support a number of animal species. Their

Above left *The leaves and seed pods of the shepherd's tree (***Boscia albitrunca***) are eaten by desert herbivores, such as the gemsbok.*
Above right *The irregular surface of* **Hoodia gordonii** *scatters the rays of the sun; the spines along its fleshy stems deter larger herbivores from eating the plant.*

seed pods provide a vital source of food for antelope, baboons and many insects. Another common tree is the wild tamarisk (*Tamarix usneoides*), occasionally found growing in thick stands to create small oases of habitat and food for other life forms. Like the lichens, the tree absorbs fog moisture and excretes salt through its leaves, an adaptation that serves as a measure of defence: the unpleasant salty residue, clearly visible on the dry leaves, is given a wide berth by browsing wildlife.

Other riverbed plants do provide food for many animals, including a variety of antelopes and far-ranging baboons lured by their leaves and fruits. Moreover, the bark and roots of the plants create microhabitats for such small invertebrates as termites and ants, which, in turn, are a source of food for scorpions, solifuges, spiders and other desert predators. In striking contrast to the life-giving fog is

Below *Blue wildebeest (**Connochaetes taurinus**), which follow the rains, graze beneath a rainbow in the Kalahari. Summer rains transform this arid savanna region from a dry desert to rich grassland for a few very short months each year.*

Right *A Kalahari lion cub cautiously takes a drink at a waterhole; its pale brown coat blends well into the desert vegetation.*

the fiercely hot east wind that blows across the plains and up the mountain valleys, drying and shrivelling everything in its way. Because there are so few animals available to disperse pollen and seeds, though, the wind is essential to the cycles of the sparse plant life: it distributes plant debris across the desert, often accumulating it in slacks and hollows that function as 'larders' for a variety of species known as detritivores (in wetter areas this role in the food chain is usually undertaken by bacteria, microorganisms and fungi). The desert detritivores include termites, ants and other insects, and lizards such as the shovel-snouted lizard (*Aporosaura anchietae*) (in central parts

of the Namib) and the lizard *Angolosaurus skoogi* (in the north). Some of the animals have specialised gut adaptations to take advantage of this unusual food source.

Since there is no ground water, many species can drink only during foggy conditions. In the early morning, the tenebrionid beetle (*Onymacris unguicularis*) adopts a posture on the crest of the dunes so that the fog condenses on its shell and runs into its mouth. The tunnelling beetle (*Lepidochora discoidalis*) has a more interesting technique: it burrows into the western (wetter) face of the coastal dunes, where condensing water collects on its back.

The Namaqua chameleon (*Chameleo namaquensis*) opens its mouth slightly to drink the moisture that runs off its body, while the sidewinding adder, also called Peringuey's adder (*Bitis peringueyi*), licks the condensing water off its own scales.

Life in the desert also requires unusual structural adaptations for mobility on the soft sands. The large white lady spider (*Carparahue avreoflava*) is a striking example: when threatened, it folds its legs under its body to cartwheel down a dune – the only animal other than man that uses the wheel principle for locomotion. One of the animals it preys upon, the gecko *Palmatogecko rangei*,

Opposite *The female pygmy falcon (**Polihierax semitorquatus**) often nests in the empty chamber of the sociable weaver's nest, but only on rare occasions will it feed on its host.*
Above *The gemsbok (**Oryx gazella**) is well adapted to life in arid climates. It can withstand very high temperatures because a network of blood vessels below its brain transfers heat away from the head to the rest of the body, so maintaining cool brain temperatures while increasing body temperature. It seeks shade but if none is available, it positions itself in a particular way in the wind so as to enhance cooling.*
Right *Sandgrouse are well known for their water-carrying abilities. They make long trips to water so as to soak their wings, and return to their nests with a few drops clinging to their bodies, which they drop into the chick's beaks.*

costume and ornamentation have been the subject of a great many magazine features, books and television documentaries.

These people – the Nama and the Ovahimba – have always lived in harmony with the desert and its fringes. Others, though, pose a growing threat to the environment. The Namib-Naukluft Park extends over more than a million hectares – a vast area that should, in theory, serve as a safe and inviolable haven for the wildlife. But many of its mammals are migratory, regularly making their way further inland

to the better grazing along the eastern borders. Here, some farmers are capitalising on the migratory urge by temporarily dismantling their fences to allow the animals to cross onto their property where they can be legally slaughtered. The roads through the park compound the threat by allowing poachers easy access. Then there is the relentless assault on the region's water resources: the beds of the Kuiseb and Swakop rivers are being plundered to help sustain the ever-growing towns of Swakopmund and Walvis Bay.

THE SANDS OF THE KALAHARI

About 300 kilometres to the east is the Kalahari; commonly termed a desert it is a region which receives a lot more rain than the

Namib (up to 500 millimetres a year in the wetter parts) and is formally classified as arid savanna. But here, as in the Namib, the rains are unreliable and localised, and storms last for very short periods. And surface water remains scarce: the sandy terrain quickly absorbs the rain, which produces a strikingly contrasting environment, one that alternates from dry desert to lush grassland. Overall, though, the Kalahari sustains a lot more vegetation than does the Namib, boasting several acacia species as well as shrubs and grasses which, when the rains are generous, grow tall.

The Kalahari Gemsbok National Park is one of South Africa's most successful sanctuaries and second in size only to the Kruger. It is bisected by the Auob and the Nossob, two large and invariably dry rivers that converge at

Below *The bat-eared fox (***Otocyon megalotis***), an omnivorous animal, lives on a diet of insects, birds, eggs, fruit and roots. It uses its large ears to detect insect prey underground.*

Twee Rivieren, a rest-camp in the southern section. Their wide beds are grazed by herds of springbok, gemsbok and other antelope.

The park in fact supports an impressive variety of big game species, many of which also occur in the savanna biome, among them lion, cheetah, leopard, jackal, hyaena, and several herbivores. The region is also known for the migrations of its herds, movements of bovids in search of water and the best grazing.

When the rains have passed and the land becomes dry once again, the animals have to find alternative sources of sustenance, and even traditional carnivores such as the hyaena may have to adopt an omnivorous diet so as to survive the drought. Here, the Kalahari's plants provide the dietary options, among them *Citrullus lanatus*, a cucurbit that grows low on the ground like a watermelon; the gemsbok cucumber (*Acanthosicyos naudinianus*), the wild cucumber (*Cucumis africanus*) and many other plant species with succulent roots and tubers that can only be reached by the determined digging of an animal or insect.

The Kalahari lions are thought to grow larger than their cousins elsewhere in southern Africa, but their kills tend to be smaller and they have to hunt more frequently. Cheetahs, specialised sprinters of the veld, also flourish on the flat grassland plains on the abundance of springbok herds. Other carnivorous animals – hyaenas, jackals, foxes – must survive on a more catholic diet.

THE LAST REFUGE

The Kalahari was home to the San (Bushmen) long before the southward migrations of the Bantu-speaking pastoralists and the much later arrival of the European colonists. Ancestral groups are thought to have occupied the region approximately 40 000 years ago; the contemporary clans in relatively recent times (about 2 000 years ago). Today, though, their unique culture, even their group identity, has all but disappeared before the onslaught of the modern state. These people have abandoned their nomadic life style in favour of a more settled existence, their age-old traditional ways no longer necessary since the advent of boreholes to provide permanent water.

Above *Despite the forbidding landscape, the Himba people of northern Namibia also manage to survive in the desert environment. Their striking looks and individual culture have attracted many journalists and anthropologists.*
Right *The nests of sociable weavers festoon many trees, and even telephone poles, in desert regions. A thick roof of straw insulates the young from the harsh rays of the sun. All of the birds in the colony cooperate in the expansion of the nest.*

The San survived and even flourished in this harsh environment by employing the most ingenious of strategies in the perennial quest for water and food. Ground moisture, for instance, was sucked from the wet sand through long reed straws; water was stored in ostrich-egg shells, which were buried deep in the remote wastelands and recovered, when needed, with uncanny accuracy even when no signs of the cache were visible. They were also adept at wringing out the juices from the stomach contents of antelope. Although bitter, these fluids are high in various nutrients and are thirst-quenching in the hot desert. Another major source of water was the tsamma melon.

For centuries, the heat and aridity of the Kalahari kept all but the San at bay and even today, as in the Namib, the forbidding nature of the land may yet prove to be its saving grace, protecting it from that destructive human encroachment that has despoiled so many of Africa's other great wildernesses.

Desert Oasis

THE OKAVANGO DELTA

The heavy summer rains of Angola's central highlands create a mighty river that rolls

into Botswana, only to die in the sands of the Kalahari. Each year a fresh surge of water feeds its delta,

replenishing one of Africa's most splendid wetland wildernesses.

The Okavango – known as the Kubango in Angola – is one of the most beautiful and idyllic of southern Africa's rivers: its banks are lined with lush growth and the occasional palm tree protruding into the air; its calmer reaches are graced by sandy banks, narrow streams and reed-lined waterholes. The water is so crystal clear that one can gaze down at its white bed, see the flash and scurry of fish and, sometimes, the dark and menacing shape of a crocodile.

But the river has another remarkable claim to notability: it never reaches the sea. Instead of flowing westwards, like the nearby Kunene and Orange rivers, it turns inland (away from the sea), running southeast to cross the Namibian panhandle of Caprivi, rush over the Popa Falls in a mighty torrent, and finally flow into the vast, flat desert land of Botswana. This journey stretches over 1 600 kilometres. As it dies in the hot sands of the Kalahari Desert, it forms one of Africa's last great wildernesses – the famed Okavango Delta.

THE SPREADING WATERS

The origin of the Okavango's unusual course is still the subject of scientific debate. One theory holds that it was once a tributary of the eastward-flowing Limpopo, another that, along with the Chobe and Zambezi rivers, it flowed into a vast lake in north-central Botswana, an

Above *The flowers of the water lily beckon passing insects, while below the water, long tough stems anchor the plant to the riverbed.*
Left *The saddle-billed stork (***Ephippiorhynchus senegalensis***) can always be seen close to water.*
Opposite *During the wet season, islands harbouring woodland and savanna are scattered like green jewels across the Delta. They are filled with game and an abundance of bird life. The largest, Chief's Island, is 100 kilometres long and 15 kilometres wide, flanked by two great tributaries, the Boro and the Santantadibe.*

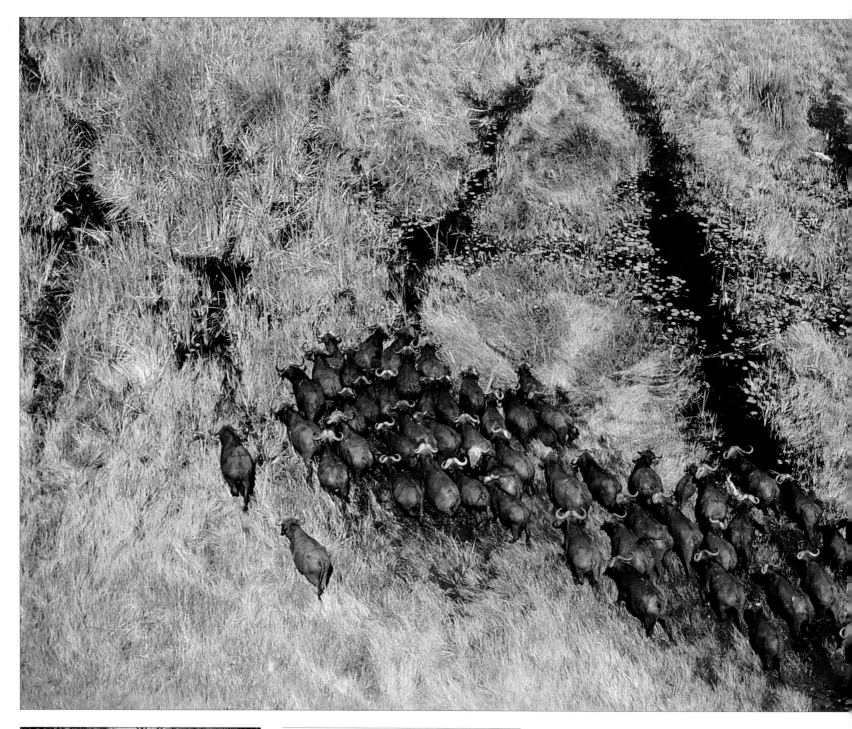

Above *The ecosystem of the Okavango revolves around the floods that dictate the lives and activities of humans and animals alike. This includes the migration of tens of thousands of antelope, buffalo and elephant, as well as the breeding cycles of many fish, birds and reptiles.*

Left *The mokoro is made from a tree that is felled and left to dry. A craftsman hollows out the trunk and shapes it into a canoe.*

inland sea that has virtually dried out to form the pans of the Makgadikgadi region. According to estimates, the lake covered between 30 000 and 80 000 square kilometres and was 100 metres deep. There is much speculation, but what is known for certain is that the geology of the area has been and is unstable, and the Okavango could well have been diverted from its original course by a movement or series of movements in the earth's crust.

single large stream, widens slightly as a result of the flatter topography and then spreads out beyond the village of Sepopa, fragmenting to fill a labyrinthine web of hitherto dry channels, riverbeds and pans. The last trickles finally make their way down the overflow into the Botletle River, to sink into the subterranean aquifers deep in the heart of the Kalahari

Below *With the exception of the mosquito-born malaria parasite, the hippopotamus is thought to have killed more humans in Africa than any other animal. Hippopotamuses are well adapted to aquatic life, and the Okavango Delta provides an ideal home. These animals can remain submerged for more than five minutes.*

Today, the Okavango fans out into a vast delta of waterways, lagoons and enchanted islands, and of flood plains that are dry for many months of the year. At the river's source, in the Angolan highlands, the rain falls from November to March and swells the river, the slow surge progressively covering the delta between June and September and transforming it into an 18 000 square kilometre wetland paradise. It crosses the Botswanan border as a

Desert. In especially bountiful years some of the water may reach the Makgadikgadi Pans, where it transforms the salt-encrusted depressions into a clear blue lake. Here, thousands of flamingos congregate to breed in the hope that their chicks will grow big enough to fly before the pans dry up again.

The people of the Okavango Delta make their way through the watery, reed-festooned terrain on dugout canoes known as *mekoro* (singular: *mokoro*). These dugouts can carry surprisingly heavy loads – several hunters with an antelope kill can easily be transported by a skilled boatman, who either sits and paddles or

stands upright, pushing a pole down and slightly backwards into the shallow bed of the channel. The boatmen have an intimate knowledge of the larger channels (and many of the smaller ones, too: those made by the regular passage of antelope), and they are remarkably skilled navigators, locating and using the shortcuts from one waterway to the next, and maintaining direction even when the route leads through reedbeds that are several kilometres wide. As they go along, they bend the stems of reeds and grasses to mark the path which, although indiscernible to outsiders, will help them find their way back again. Throughout the journey, and when they disembark or climb into their craft, they keep an eye open for crocodile and hippopotamus which resent intrusion, especially when there are calves around.

THE OKAVANGO'S ANIMALS

The Delta is home to a diversity of wildlife, supporting 540 different kinds of bird, 157 reptiles, 164 mammals, 80 fish species, and 5 000 insect species. But the numbers are not as striking as the images conveyed to and remembered by the visitor – a phalanx of buffalo seeking the area's rich grazing and abundant waters, for instance; hippopotamus wallowing among the papyrus beds and the unmistakeable cry of the African fish eagle.

Then there are the species specially adapted for life in this watery world, among them the elusive sitatunga *(Tragelaphus spekei)*, an antelope that has evolved splayed hooves of up to 18 centimetres long, which enable it to spread its weight over a wide area of wet ground; and the lechwe *(Kobus lechwe)*, which is related to the better-known waterbuck *(Kobus ellipsiprymnus)*. Waterbuck, in fact, can swim as proficiently as the sitatunga although they lack the splayed hooves.

The Delta provides ideal living conditions for the Nile crocodile *(Crocodylus niloticus)*, a reptile that is ranked among the earth's most successful predators – it has survived unchanged in form and habit for millions of years.

Below left and right *The sitatunga (right) is well adapted to Delta life. This beautiful creature has a dense coat and slightly spiralled horns, and is an extremely good swimmer. It is known to hide in the water with only its nostrils visible above the surface until danger has passed. On the marshy banks, its broad hooves prevent it from sinking deep into the mud. Another aquatically adapted antelope is the red lechwe (left) – also a competent swimmer.*

The animal's favoured hunting patch is, usually, in the water close to the bank, where it lurks half-submerged, only its eyes and nostrils protruding above the surface. There it waits, motionless for hours until an unwary creature strays within striking distance, when it lunges with a rapid flick of its powerful tail.

Sharing the habitat, but definitely no friend of the crocodile, is the hippopotamus (*Hippopotamus amphibius*), a massive mammal intimately associated with water but which, during dry periods, will wander far afield in search of fresh grazing. While in the water, hippopotamuses have no natural enemies, though as the Delta dries out each year they are forced to move from pool to pool and are vulnerable to predators during their overland journeys. Many other large mammals, elephant and buffalo among them, congregate around the pans and lakelets that mark the outer limits of this freshwater system.

BIRDS OF THE DELTA

The Okavango Delta is a wonderland of birds, hosting an abundance of such beautiful species as the malachite kingfisher (*Alcedo cristata*) and pied kingfisher (*Ceryle rudis*). Both of these hunt from perches that overhang the channels and lagoons. Then there is the elegant darter (*Anhinga melanogaster*), which moves swiftly and silently through the water, looking much like a swimming snake (it is known locally as the 'snake-bird'), striking at its prey with its dagger-like bill. The bird is similar in many respects to its relative, the reed cormorant (*Phalacrocorax africanus*): both species have long necks which enable them to dart at their prey with lightning speed. Unlike many other aquatic birds, the coarse plumage of the cormorant is not fully waterproof and must be dried periodically by the bird spreading its wings to the sun while perched.

Other fishing birds include the egrets and herons, all of which hunt from above, plunging their heads through the water's surface in their invariably successful efforts to catch fish, frogs and insect larvae. The African jacana (*Actophilornic africanus*) is adapted to life on the water, its extra-long toes and nails spreading its weight over the mosaic of disc-shaped lilies while it struts around in search of small aquatic insects; it supplements its diet with small frogs and tadpoles.

Above *The unmistakable call of the African fish eagle has become a symbol of the African wilderness. Closely related to the American bald eagle (*Haliaeetus leucocephalus*), this bird feeds in a similar way by snatching fish from the water's surface after a swooping dive.*

The hamerkop (*Scopus umbretta*) is one of the Delta's more distinctive residents, an unusual-looking bird with a broad bill and a tuft of feathers at the back of its head, the whole shape somewhat reminiscent of a hammer (hence the name). It also feeds on frogs and insects, and builds large, distinctive dome-shaped nests in trees along the river banks. Many other birds, each with its own method of feeding, live among the waterways, but none has so enchanting a call as the African fish eagle (*Haliaeetus vocifer*), one of only a few eagles adapted to an aquatic diet (its much rarer Madagascar cousin, *Haliaeetus vociferoides*, is another) although it will also take terrestrial prey such as other birds, small mammals and reptiles. It is at its most efficient when swooping down over the water to impale, with its long, sharp, tough talons, an unsuspecting fish that has ventured too close to the surface.

THE SMALLER LIFE FORMS

The Delta's larger animals are the most immediately eye-catching, but its waters also teem with a myriad smaller forms of life. At night the air is filled with the cacophony of frogs of various kinds, each calling its territory among the reedbeds. They include species of the genus *Hyperolius*, which are agile climbers and prodigious jumpers. Another, more curious inhabitant is the foam-nest tree-frog (*Chiromantis xerampelina*), which is an exceptional climber, its fingers and toes equipped with discs that enable it to cling to vertical surfaces.

These frogs can withstand long periods out of the water by secreting and covering themselves with a waterproof layer of mucus. They are masters of camouflage, able to change their colours from a dark grey to almost white. Their most interesting characteristic, though, involves their reproductive cycle: members of this genus lay their eggs in a mass of froth deposited on the vegetation that overhangs the water; dense growth that protects the nest from aquatic predators. About five days after the eggs have been laid, the tadpoles will fall through the frothy mass and into the water.

By day, dragonflies and damselflies of all colours can be seen along the banks, guarding their territories or perching motionless on overhanging twigs and papyrus strands. Dragonfly nymphs (juveniles), which perch on submerged sections of papyrus, are predatory, lying in wait for small passing insects, fish and young tadpoles before climbing above the surface to emerge as high-speed aviators.

Fishing spiders prey on small aquatic life, floating on its surface but tethered to the bank by a strand of silk. As small fish and tadpoles swim up to investigate a potential meal, the spider lunges below the water to inflict its lethal bite. Fish such as the widespread African tilapia, catfish and the predatory tiger fish (*Hydrocynus vittatus*), which is much prized by sporting anglers, find a plentiful supply of food in this environment and are, in turn, a source of food for many birds.

The thick plant growth along the borders of the river is more than just a home to the wildlife: the papyrus beds play an important ecological role by filtering the water carried down the river. The beds stabilise the banks, enabling such trees as water-rooted figs to mature. In slower-moving waters, scented lily flowers splash colour across a green tapestry of leaves; occasionally, where the flow is faster, rafts of papyrus break away from the bank to drift gently downstream.

PARADISE UNDER THREAT

The first people to settle in the Delta region, about 2 000 years ago, were the baNoka (or River Bushmen), their presence here illustrated by the many paintings and engravings to

Frogs of the Delta

*Painted reed frogs (*Hyperolius marmoratus*) can be found in various colour forms throughout the Delta's waters. Some individuals are striped black, white, yellow and red, while others may appear blotched or spotted. Their underparts are usually pale, or bright pink. These amphibians change colour according to sex and age, and also in response to local environmental conditions, such as habitat and exposure to sunlight. The limbs of many frogs are adapted to grasp onto thin, reedy vegetation along the banks of the waterways. These limbs are useful during mating (below) when the male grasps and holds the female until she releases her eggs, which he can then fertilise immediately with his sperm.*

Above left *African jacanas (**Actophilornis africanus**) – also known as 'Lily-trotters' – are able to walk on the leaves of lilies floating on the water.*
Above right *Thick banks of papyrus provide a food source and habitat for many forms of invertebrate life; below the water, a tangle of stems acts as a nursery for juvenile fish.*
Below left *Various dragonflies of all colours thrive in the shallow reedbeds of the Delta.*
Below right *A game fence around the Delta now separates a wilderness from the encroachment of mankind and his livestock.*

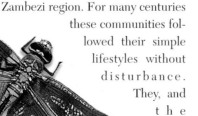

be seen in the nearby Tsodilo Hills. These people originally used papyrus rafts, from which they fished, but later adapted to the *mokoro*. Other Delta inhabitants arrived much later: the baYei and HaMbukushu, fisherfolk, hunters and farmers from the Zambezi region. For many centuries these communities followed their simple lifestyles without disturbance. They, and the

animals and plants of this magical wetland, were left in peace – until the economic imperatives of modern society intruded. The pressures are now so severe that the future of this ecosystem hangs in the balance. Here, in the largely arid Kalahari, the most valuable commodity is not mineral wealth or ivory, but fresh water, and the Delta's vast resources are jealously eyed by a number of interests – notably the cattle-ranching and mining industries.

While the Delta itself has no valuable minerals to speak of, extensive diamond deposits occur further south, at Orapa in the Kalahari Desert – and the extraction process needs large quantities of water to wash off sand and gravel in order to recover the valuable stones. Since 1971 the mining industry has dredged from several localities in the Delta, notably the Boro River – which is one of the main channels – and this proved disastrous for the wildlife in certain areas: migrating animals arrived at the traditional pans only to find them dry. Plans for further dredging have now been shelved pending an environmental impact assessment.

Currently, most of the water for the mines comes from boreholes, which impacts on the underground water tables and surrounding pans. One alternative approach that seems to have merit proposes that water be piped to around the Delta from the north – using an environment-friendly solar pump. Such a

reticulation system would allow normal flooding, create no barriers, and therefore would not interfere with the sediment inflow because the effects of water loss would be spread over the entire Okavango Delta.

The threat from mining is, given the nature of the industry, a temporary one. A far greater danger is that posed by cattle ranching, one that holds profound and far-reaching consequences and will affect the Delta in many ways. Certain areas are home to the tsetse fly, to which the wildlife is immune but the cattle vulnerable. Pesticides are being used, sometimes on a wide scale, and regular spraying has been cited as one reason for the decreasing wildlife populations of the Delta. Birds are especially at risk, for pesticides such as DDT weaken the shells of their eggs, causing excessive chick mortality.

Even more devastating to the environment are the various fences erected to control the cattle and the wildlife, and to inhibit the spread of foot-and-mouth disease. The fences are death traps for migratory game. Here, though, the argument that Botswana's resources are for its people, and not exclusively for the delight of overseas visitors, is one that cannot easily be ignored.

Poachers also continue to take a heavy toll, and operate with virtual impunity – they know the area quite well and can easily escape into the reedy channels. Again, many of them are ordinary villagers who often have little to eat and are merely seeking to supplement their diet, which gives the issue a very human, and sensitive, dimension.

The Delta is said to be an ecotourism destination that really works, because it pays its way and does not rely on government funding. But if it works too well – if too many visitors arrive – the character and ecology of the area will suffer. Where once there was unspoiled wilderness, hotels do brisk business and motorboats ply the channels. The local inhabitants do not gain much reward from the influx of tourists: a few individuals are employed as polers and guides, but they earn a pittance.

Yet one should not underestimate the lobbying power of the ecotourism industry and the benefits it can bring to conservation. Had the region not been an internationally recognised destination, most of its water would probably by now have been surrendered to mining and cattle ranching interests.

However, it is now imperative that the Okavango Delta be declared a world heritage site – a move that, although it will not solve the problems overnight, will at least involve the international community in the struggle to rescue this great wetland wilderness.

Right *Pel's fishing owl (***Scotopelia peli***) is a nocturnal hunter along the tributaries of the Delta. Although difficult to see, this owl's eerie call can be heard at night from very far off. It hunts like the fish eagle, swooping down and grasping prey from the water's surface with its long talons. It has elongated and spiney toes which enable it to grasp slippery fish.*

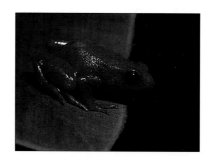

Land of the Ancestors

MADAGASCAR'S TROPICAL FORESTS

*At the **northeastern** tip of Madagascar lies one of the world's most*

important and fascinating rainforests, home to plants and animals that are found nowhere

else. But, like tropical forests elsewhere, it is under serious threat.

Madagascar, rising dramatically above the warm, blue Indian Ocean, 400 kilometres from Africa's southeastern coast, is the world's fourth largest island. This beautiful island covers approximately 600 000 square kilometres of rugged, high, deeply ravined countryside and, because of its size, its different elevations and its great longitudinal range, it embraces an astonishing variety of natural environments.

The central highlands separate the drier western areas from the wetter eastern ones; the southern region is semi-arid, with some parts receiving as little as 300 millimetres of rain in a year; the northeastern segment of the island has a tropical climate, its Masoala Peninsula receiving more than 4 000 millimetres of rain per year and supporting lush and rich rainforests, here at the southern limit of their range.

The Masoala Peninsula is more or less pear-shaped, projecting southwards into a coral sea. Bordered in the west by the Baie d' Antongil, and by the warm waters of the ocean on the east, it is a relatively pristine region. This is largely because of the Peninsula's remoteness as well as the protective mountain range that runs along its western side.

THE HIDDEN WORLD

Seen from the air, the land is mantled by a vast, monochromatic blanket of foliage that obscures all detail below. But beneath the dense canopy lies a secret world in which a great multitude of plants and animals has

Above *The golden mantella (***Mantella aurantiaca***) is one of the Masoala rainforest's most striking amphibious inhabitants.*
Left *The Madagascar boa (***Sanzinia madagascariensis***) is one of the forest's larger predators.*
Opposite *Lush tropical forests once covered large areas of eastern Madagascar; 90 per cent of its plant species are endemic to the island.*

survived and flourished in evolutionary exile – aeons ago the island cut loose from the African mainland, and its species have followed their own Darwinian paths. Many of those recorded are found nowhere else; others have yet to be identified. Splendidly large trees rise majestically, thrusting their crowns into the emerald mantle above, while vines and lianas dangle in profusion from their branches down to the ground. Wild orchids provide visual relief in the green-and-brown dimness with their

Below The forest understorey in reserves such as this one in Perinet hosts countless plant and animal species, many undescribed by science.
Right *Many reptiles, such as snakes and geckos, can be found in Masoala's tropical forests. The genus* **Phelsuma** *consists of geckos that are active during the day; these have evolved cryptic colours with green shades to elude their predators, and the most impressive is the widespread day gecko (***Phelsuma madagascariensis***).*

brilliant splashes of colour; strange fruits that resemble outgrowths of fungus burst from the bark of the tree-trunks; dead and decaying leaves, thick moss and scatters of ferns occupy patches of the forest floor, and the quiet air is filled with mysterious scents, and with the sound of the forest birds, of frogs, and of the countless insects. Occasionally, a lemur can be heard calling from a distance.

Not all plant life is confined to the forest floor. Epiphytes, which include many of the orchids, live on other plants high above the ground, preyed on by such insect herbivores as beetles, caterpillars and bugs – the whole community, plants and animals, combining to form a coherent ecological system that is both extra-

ordinarily intricate and superbly balanced. Predation, or the lack of it, has determined the characteristics of many of the plants and animals. Because this kind of tropical forest lacks the large herbivores that occur in larger rainforest regions elsewhere, few trees have evolved thorns, although some have a prickly bark that may inhibit the movement of such fruit-eating animals as lemurs. Other defensive mechanisms abound. In a spectacular display of natural selection, for instance, the body and tail of the leaf-tailed gecko (*Uroplatus fimbriatus*) have evolved to enable the lizard to flatten itself, and remain invisible, flush against the trunk of a tree. It spends most of its day clinging, often upside-down, to the bark.

Left *The brown lemur (***Lemur fulvis fulvis***), the most common of all Madagascar's lemurs, lives in a variety of habitats.*
Above *A paper wasp of the* **Belonogaster** *genus prepares its nest, which is often built below an overhanging rock near water.*

THE NEVER-ENDING CYCLE

In tropical forests, the processes of growth and decay are quicker than in any other earth environment. But like rainforests elsewhere, the growth and decay processes of the Masoala Peninsula are remarkably stable in terms of moisture and temperature. The wet climate provides ideal habitats for a huge diversity of invertebrates, including the familiar millipedes, centipedes and giant terrestrial isopods (woodlice and other flat-bodied bugs). The high humidity levels also, as noted, nurture a variety of lichens and mosses, which grow on all the surfaces touched by light. Many of them absorb moisture directly from the air. The stability of this ancient ecosystem depends on the large trees of the canopy, a sun-blocking

barrier formed by the upper branches and the vegetation that grows on them. The forest floor receives little light, and thus supports relatively few plants: there is little undergrowth, and one can make one's way through the forest easily. But when a tree falls and dies, it creates a window in the canopy, and although young saplings will grow, eventually to fill the gap, the sun-filled patch will temporarily sustain a thick growth. The fallen tree-trunk itself becomes home to many insect species and to some unusual forms of life, such as bracket fungi and other wood-rotting species.

The soil has limited nutritional value because most minerals and organic materials are locked up in the tissues of the trees themselves. It is essential to the survival of the ecosystem, therefore, that these nutrients be returned to the soil periodically in order to sustain the various cycles of life. One of the

most important recycling stages is the breaking down of wood by termites, which build their nests in fallen logs. The process is taken further by many ants that carry away bits and pieces of the decaying tree (and, incidentally, help in the dispersal of seeds).

Despite the lack of vegetation, the forest floor supports a vast concourse of other creatures. Snails (of which Madagascar has more than 380 identified species) are slow-moving scavengers that break down the abundant organic material that falls to the ground.

The moist environment is also ideal for amphibians, such as frogs, some of which are adapted to laying their eggs away from permanent water. This adaptation enables them to take advantage of the rich supply of forest insects on which they feed. Many of the frogs have no need of camouflage: they display bright colours that warn potential predators of the poisonous compounds within their skin. Even crabs have colonised the rainforest.

THE CREATURES OF THE FOREST

Madagascar is home to more than 60 different types of snake but, because dangerous snakes such as the front-fanged adders, vipers and

Above and right: *The leaf-tailed gecko's broad, flattened feet grip the bark of a tree. A wide frill along the edge of its body enables it to blend its outline with its surroundings. It can change its colours to match the surface on which it is resting, thus remaining almost invisible to the birds and snakes that prey on it. When touched, it startles its attacker by abruptly changing its appearance. It can also lose its tail, leaving a tasty morsel to divert the predator long enough for it to escape.*

cobras of Africa never evolved in this long-isolated land, the island has no dangerous snakes. Snakes smell with their tongues and pick up the vibrations of their prey through their bodies – acute senses which enable them

to stalk slowly, noiselessly and relentlessly across the forest floor. There are innumerable different habitats in this timeless and fragile ecosystem, each one home to a very different collection of creatures. Small streams and creeks flow among the great trees, carrying water to the neighbouring ocean, and give life to many animals that cannot live else-where. The frogs they sustain are agile swim-mers, as well as excellent jumpers, but they prefer fast-flowing watercourses into which they can escape. The creeks also provide open spaces above the water for orb-web spiders to construct their webs, some of which can span as much as 15 metres.

The streams on the western side of the Masoala Peninsula are fed by the ever-present clouds above the steep mountain slopes.

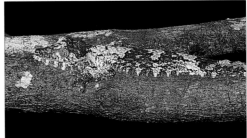

Grand Masters of Camouflage

Among the most interesting inhabitants of Madagascar, apart from its lemurs, are its chameleons of which there is an extraordinary diversity. More than two-thirds of the world's chameleon species are found here.

Chameleons are solitary reptiles which do not resemble any other type of lizard. Their conical eyes move independently to survey their surroundings for danger, but focus together when prey is in sight. Males are often more brightly coloured than females and may have horns or other ornamentation such as elongated casques on their heads, which are used as jousting pieces during head-to-head combat.

The most remarkable feature of these reptiles is their ability to change colour so as to blend with their immediate surroundings. Some of their most striking and vivid colour changes occur when they are either courting females or when involved in a territorial dispute with a neighbour and not, as is commonly believed, when they move to different surroundings. They have a prehensile tail, coiled up when not in use, that functions as a strong, fifth 'hand' used to aid movement. The tail and the grasping feet enable the chameleons on this island to move with ease through the forest understorey.

Further downstream, nearer the coast, the creeks are girded by mangroves whose roots project above the soil, spreading wide to support the trees in the swampy ground. Some mangrove tree species have specialised aerial roots hanging down from the branches, an adaptation that keeps them from becoming waterlogged in the intertidal habitat.

Underwater, among the roots and above the fertile mud, various creatures survive on forest-derived detritus, such as leaves and other plant material that sinks to the bottom or remains suspended in the water.

Madagascar has few indigenous freshwater fish. Many mangrove species are of marine origin: they breed in the tidal forests, where their young have plenty of food and have the advantage of a much less rigorous environment than the open sea. When they reach maturity, the fish leave through the mouth of the estuary.

The forest's magnificent trees stop the life-giving sun from entering the damp and shadowy world below, yet they support animated communities far above the forest floor. Unlike the forest communities of Central America, where scientists have long been active, life in the higher strata of the Masoala forest canopy is virtually unknown. But it is known that a number of insect species live exclusively in this habitat, where many bird species also spend much of their time. This elevated domain is the least explored part of the tropical rainforest, and it undoubtedly harbours a wealth of as yet unnamed species of insects and plants.

LIVING FOSSILS

Better known, larger but still elusive creatures also find safety and shelter in the canopy – most notably the lemurs, a group of about 30 species of primates that belong to a mammalian order found only in Madagascar. Before the evolution of modern primates – the monkeys and apes – lemurs were spread widely across what are now the different continents. When Madagascar drifted off from Gondwanaland, it became a type of Noah's Ark, a haven for animals that, more than 40 million years ago, managed to bridge the channel to the island by rafting on branches and logs. The ancestral lemurs have long since disappeared in other parts of the world, victims of the

larger predators and of unequal competition with modern primates. In the largely predator-free isolation of Madagascar, however, they survived and flourished, evolving into a number of different species. Some, like the golden bamboo lemur (*Hapalemur aureus*) have only recently been identified (in 1987), and a number of experts believe that there are still areas where unknown species await discovery. The indri (*Indri indri*) is Madagascar's largest surviving lemur. Its song is territorial, serving to mark out an area for a specific family group, which normally consists of between two and five individuals. The species is ideally adapted for life in the forest: its limbs are remarkable for their suppleness; its feet are hand-like, able to grasp fairly thick branches; and its eyes have

Above *Large tracts of lowland forest on the eastern coastal plateau have now given way to rice fields.*

Right *The tenrec is one of the strangest mammals in the forest. Some species have modified hairs in the form of protective bristles which can produce a high-pitched rattling noise to startle prospective predators; they also play a role in communication. An unkempt-looking creature, it uses its long snout to search for prey.*

a reflective retina that enhances vision in the dim light of the forest. Indris travel from tree to tree in a series of prodigious leaps, hurtling as much as ten metres through the branches in their search for food. According to one

Malagasy legend, it was this lemur that gave rise to humans: the folk story tells of an ancient time when an indri gave birth to two sons, one of whom remained in the trees while the other took to a bipedal life on the ground.

THE COMING OF MAN

For millions of years the lemurs were the only primates in this island paradise. But isolation was not to last. Some 2 000 years ago humans came, initially from Malaysia and Polynesia, and from Indonesia, and finally from Africa, bringing with them tools, weapons, the knowledge of fire and farming. In a fraction of the time that it took for the island's unique life forms to evolve, these people changed the face of this ancient land. Many of the new arrivals penetrated the interior by river, while others settled in the highlands. As their numbers grew, they began to make inroads into the forest and to overburden its resources. They needed land on which to grow the rice which

Below left The local people regard chameleons with suspicion. They believe these lizards to be inhabited by powerful spirits that keep one eye on the past and the other on the future.
Below right The Madagascar boa is a non-venomous constrictor that kills its prey by wrapping its coils around it and squeezing tightly. Its ability to unhinge its jaw enables it to swallow its food whole.

their immigrant forefathers had brought from Asia; today the crop is cultivated in even the remotest parts of the country, including the Peninsula. Rice production poses an enormous threat to the ecology because its cultivation requires large surface areas, and it eventually exhausts the nutrient-poor soil. Low-lying, flat forest areas are especially suitable for the crop, which is one reason why the rugged mountain forests on the western side of the Masoala Peninsula have so far been spared. When African immigrants brought cattle, which need even larger tracts of land for grazing, the pressures on the forests intensified. These farming practices are highly productive in the short term, but once the soil has been degraded the compulsion is to clear even more areas of forest. The larger trees are felled and the undergrowth hacked down. When the ground has dried out, it is scorched – a destructive process of slash-and-burn known locally as 'tavy'. Sometimes the largest trees survive, but in the coastal regions they are at a premium since the local people fashion their fishing boats from their trunks. More than 90 per cent of Madagascar's indigenous forests have been lost – and many once-unique species have disappeared. The future of the remaining forests,

and the plants and animals they support, is now in serious jeopardy. When vegetation is destroyed, the high rainfall in the tropics quickly leaches the soil and so, with the destruction of the forests, the very survival of the most successful primates, humans, is threatened. Sheer numbers are at the root of the problem: once an exporter of rice, Madagascar now has to import grain to feed its rapidly growing population. The country has one of the world's fastest growing human populations; half the residents are under 15 years of age. Habitat destruction, combined with hunting, has driven one-third of all modern lemur species to extinction; 14 types of lemur have disappeared. There are no certain or complete solutions to these profound environmental problems, but a lot can be done to minimise the impact of degradation.

First, the local community's dependence on rice has to be changed in favour of more ecologically friendly crops. Sweet potatoes and other tubers have far less effect on the forest ecology. Then there are export commodities such as vanilla, a vine-like plant which is cultivated intensively and can be harvested year after year without disturbing the soil. Unfortunately, Madagascar's vanilla industry is

Below *People still venture into the remaining patches of forest in search of medicinal plants that are used as traditional remedies.*
Right *The area around villages is often cleared of its large trees for fire wood or building material.*

currently tightly controlled by a small group and brings very little benefit to the local people. Much of the tropical forest's potential remains untapped. With such high species diversity, novel food plants may well exist in the still mysterious depths.

A large segment of the Masoala Peninsula's forest area was recently set aside as a national park, but unless the local community is assured that it will gain from the scheme, it is doomed to failure: people will simply ignore pleas for proper resource management. New and innovative ways to spread the benefits of conservation need to be explored.

Solutions that satisfy conservationists and locals alike are never easy to find, and many are politically contentious. If these last remaining forests are to be saved, it is imperative that the goal of sustainable development be achieved so that the people will not have to leave their land in search of a better future.

Paradise under Pressure

THE TROPICAL COASTS

Extending across a wide belt on either side of the

equator lies a conspicuous, highly distinctive biological community,

known as a coral reef.

The warm, shallow coastal waters of the tropics are home to massive reefs of coral – brilliantly hued submarine hills and ridges created over the millennia from the accumulated remains of countless tiny organisms. The reefs form delicate necklaces around many of the oceanic islands and, in some regions – notably along the northeastern Australian coast – gird the great landmasses. Viewed from a distance they may seem incapable of sustaining a great deal of life, but in fact they are complete ecosystems, rivalling the lushest of the terrestrial regions in the diversity of their species. The reef lying off Madagascar's Masoala Peninsula, for instance, nurtures as many living forms as that island's famed rainforest. And just as the forests of the land are sustained by the life-giving qualities of the sun, so the coral reefs are the ultimate product of solar radiation. Tropical seas are relatively poor in nutrients, unable to support many of the more complex creatures – those creatures on the higher links of the food chain – but sunlight penetrates the clear blue waters, and one group of organisms, the corals, has evolved by tapping into this boundless source of neverending energy.

It is these corals – primitive multicellular animals – that form both the physical and ecological basis of an entire ecosystem, stretching to depths of as much as 50 metres in warm, coastal waters throughout the world.

Above *The resources of southern African coral reefs, particularly those of Madagascar, are now under threat as the country's rapidly growing population demands more protein resources.*

Left *The lion or devil fish (of the **Pterois** genus) is protected by spines which carry highly toxic venom. This fish species occurs throughout the Indian Ocean in association with sheltered reefs.*

Right *From Cape Vidal northwards along the east coast of southern Africa, and surrounding the island of Madagascar, water temperatures of the Indian Ocean are high enough to encourage the formation of coral reefs.*

Above *A well-camouflaged octopus (***Octopus vulgaris***) can change colour instantly and assume the texture of the background surroundings. It can pass through openings large enough to let its head through and can, therefore, conceal itself in the smallest of crevices. The octopus secretes an inky substance that confuses its pursuer as to its hiding place.*

Left *The underwater world of the coral reef projects tranquillity and calm. A honeycomb stingray (***Himantura varnak***) glides peacefully across the landscape, propelling itself with gentle undulating movements.*

Opposite *Not all corals contain photosynthetic alga or build calcarious reefs. The soft corals occur throughout the world in a very wide variety of colours and forms and are often found growing in deeper waters and caves where no light can penetrate.*

HALF PLANT, HALF ANIMAL

Corals are tiny animals closely related to anemones. They live together in clusters, each individual – known as a polyp – connected to its neighbour by tiny strands that extend laterally. The colony develops as new polyps form, often from these connecting sections, in a continuous process, their skeletons growing over the older polyps and stifling them. With reef-building corals the little colonial animals secrete calcium carbonate, which forms a hard, encasing skeleton, creating the myriad structures, each of which is distinctive of its kind, into which they retreat for safety during the day. The key to their success is the incorporation of algal cells – miniscule plants known as algae – into their own tissues, which enables them to photosynthesise food from the sun during the day. Both the algae and the corals are able to live without the other but their relationship is mutually beneficial, enabling them to thrive in the nutrient-poor, shallow waters.

At night, though, the corals assume a quite different life-style. No longer behaving like harmless plants, these tiny colonial animals become predators to feed indiscriminately on plankton. Their stinging, multi-tentacled mouths sway in the current, each polyp reaching out to numerous microscopic organisms that venture close to it.

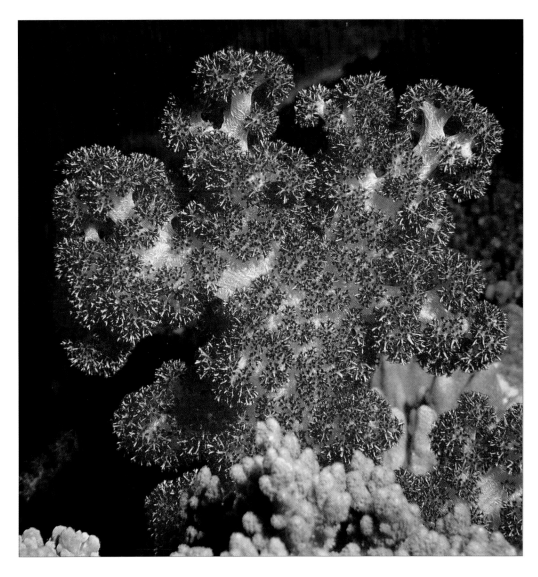

THE MAKING OF MOUNTAINS

Corals are the building blocks of a far larger system. As we have noted, their skeletons expand continuously, the lime structures sometimes growing large enough to form an offshore wall. This rampart, or reef, often acts as a barrier against the various pressures of the open ocean, elements such as the currents and tides, which would otherwise disturb the ocean floor and destroy the clarity of the water.

Behind the reef, and protected from the ocean, an entire underwater universe flourishes in kaleidoscopic fashion. The beautiful coral creates the environment for a bewildering diversity of marine species, serving as the bedrock on and around which unrelated creatures lead independent lives while using the coral for shelter and food.

Broad expanses of sea-grasses, well protected from the ferocity of the open ocean, cover the floor of many lagoons like lush green carpets, converting the sun's energy, through photosynthesis, into oxygen and sugars and then releasing nutrients into the lagoon when they decay. Sea-grasses are the only seed plants to flourish in these tropical waters.

The nutrients in the sea-grass, and in the silt deposits, invite even stranger creatures. Among these are the slow-moving sea cucumbers, some species of which can be up to a metre long and which function as the vacuum cleaners of the ecological system. As they drag themselves across the ocean floor, very small nutritious particles stick to their tentacles, which are bent inwards to feed their gaping mouths. When disturbed, sea cucumbers sometimes disembowel themselves so that long strings of sticky gut hang outside their bodies. This strange behaviour is poorly understood, though the evolutionary rationale could be that it is better for the species to surrender its gut to a predator than risk its whole body being torn apart. Or there might be another reason altogether: the inverted gut of many species is shiny white, sticky and rather alien-looking, which may repel the sea cucumber's antagonist. Whatever the motivation, the mechanism seems to work well enough: the sea cucumber has the ability to regenerate its innards, and invariably makes a full recovery.

PREDATOR AND PREY

The hunt and kill plays as important a role in the life of the coral reef system as it does in the rainforests or any other of Africa's natural environments. Among marine predators are a variety of fishes, including sharks, that frequent the lagoons and outer fringes of the reefs. Although potential man-eating sharks rarely venture into the lagoons themselves, reef sharks and other members of the Class Chondrichthyes, such as guitar fishes and rays, are common within the reef system. Many are structurally adapted to the conditions, possessing attributes that enable them to locate and catch their prey. Guitar fishes have markedly flattened bodies, which are ideal for moving in very shallow water without drawing attention

Slow-moving puffer fish are avoided due to their deadly poisonous skin and intestines, and can also inflate their bodies to intimidate potential predators (some brandish spines). The torpedo ray (*Torpedo sinuspersici*) has little to fear – it can deliver a powerful electric shock that discourages most would-be attackers. This capability – the product of the electric field it has created – is also used as a kind of radar to locate and immobilise its own prey.

The octopus is a master of camouflage and deceit, confusing and shaking off pursuers by ejecting an inky substance to cloud the water.

to themselves. The mouth is located on the ventral side, helping them to feed on the crabs and other crustaceans of the grassy plain or sandy bottom between the coral outcrops.

Other species in this predator-and-prey environment have evolved a variety of defensive shapes and habits. Some species boast highly effective camouflage, others the ability to dig themselves quickly into the ocean floor, still others tend to 'freeze' when they are disturbed, thus remaining virtually indistinguishable from their surroundings.

This species is also a clever predator, lying in wait for the crustaceans and other creatures that comprise its diet. The octopus uses all eight tentacles to pounce upon the prey. The octopus roams effortlessly between the surface and the ocean floor, cruising at any preferred speed in search of food. Octopuses are molluscs, and closely related to the humble snail, although they have lost their shells and developed a number of special capabilities: they move through the water, for example, by means of a jet-propulsion mechanism.

Above left *The bluestreak cleaner wrasse* (**Labroides dimidiatus**) *is a gregarious species which with its bright colours serves to attract other fish to cleaning stations that exist on the reef.* **Above** *A juvenile emperor angelfish* (**Pomacanthus imperator**) *cruises alongside a coral head in the clear waters of the reef. Adult fish* (**right**) *are equally colourful but look entirely different. Many reef fish will change both colour and sex as they mature. The transition is usually (but not always) from male to female, since a larger size enables bigger clutches of eggs to be produced.*

MUTUAL RELATIONSHIPS

Some inhabitants of the coral reef system have evolved even more bizarre habits by maintaining beneficial relationships with other and often dangerous creatures. The cleaner wrasse, for example, scours and eats the parasites from the scales of a variety of much larger species. These fish, usually no longer than a few centimetres, are electric blue in colour, so that they are easily recognisable by potential partners seeking a thorough (and health-giving)

cleaning. And they enhance their profile even further by associating with other members of their species, each moving around the others in sweeping movements within a small area to advertise a kind of 'cleaning station'.

The ultimate underwater defence, as many skin divers know to their cost, is a barricade of long spines designed to keep intruders at bay. Those of the sea urchin can inflict a painful, burning wound, particularly when the spine breaks off inside the victim's flesh. On Madagascar's Masoala Peninsula the tradi-

tional and very effective treatment is to rub green papaya on the wound and then beat the affected area with a stick to break up the pieces of spine in the victim's flesh – the acids in the papaya's sap prevent infection.

A BALANCED ECOSYSTEM

The reef area is a finely balanced ecosystem made up of many components – a balance maintained within an intricate web of predator and prey relationships. The network is infinitely complex. Several fish species, for example eat urchins, which keeps their numbers at optimum levels (the urchin populations would otherwise grow uncontrollably large). Most urchins graze on algae; one – the 'crown of thorns' – feeds on the coral itself, and can destroy the entire reef if it is allowed to proliferate. Other fish keep the reefs clean by using

their sharp, elongated snouts to suck up detritus and algae from the coral, thus helping the tiny colonial animals to function properly. Without their intervention, silt, detritus and algae would soon smother the reef, so preventing photosynthesis. Other species are adapted to feed on the coral itself, among them the parrot fish (of the *Scarus* genus) (so called for its bright colours, and because its teeth have grown together into an upper and lower pair, an arrangement resembling a parrot's beak). These and other elements need to function properly to ensure that the coral reef system remains in a state of equilibrium.

MARINE REPTILES AND MAMMALS

Turtles are among the few reptiles which have adapted to live in a marine environment, though their emancipation from the land is not

complete: in some instances, they migrate thousands of kilometres to find suitable terrestrial nesting sites. As many as five turtle species can be found in the Indo-Pacific region.

Turtles are endangered everywhere in the world, either because their nesting sites are destroyed by coastal development or the adults and their eggs are regarded as sought-after delicacies. Many turtles, too, get entangled in coastal nets and die; others swallow pieces of plastic floating in the ocean (the flotsam is mistaken for jellyfish, clogging up the animal's digestive system).

Among marine mammals found along the tropical coasts is the dugong (*Dugong dugon*), an animal that is sometimes, and aptly, termed a sea cow. Its diet consists only of sea-grass, and though it can hide in the open ocean during the day, it has to make night-time forays into the shallow waters where the grasses grow.

These animals are seriously threatened, and have become very rare in the Indo-Pacific region. Dolphins are sometimes found in lagoons but occur more often in the open sea.

THE COMING OF A SUPER-PREDATOR

About 2 000 years ago a super-predator appeared on the Masoala Peninsula, disturbing forever the tranquillity of its underwater world.

From the first, the settlers relied heavily on the sea for their protein requirements. Initially this did not create many environmental problems: traditional fishing methods – the woven reed-traps, for instance – rarely depleted the resources; villagers caught only what they needed for the day, and for centuries the communities supported themselves without exhausting the fruits of the sea.

But increasing human numbers has intensified the pressures. Underwater traps are still placed at the bottom of lagoons, as are traditional spears to kill and gather a variety of marine species, but there are now too many people relying on the sea for their livelihood.

As a result of the growing population, large and sprawling towns have sprung up near the Masoala Peninsula. More people means that

Opposite *The coral rock cod (*Cephalopholis miniata*) is a territorial hunter, lurking in hollows in the reef until prey passes by.*
Below *Groupers are among the largest reef fish. The yellow fin grouper (*Epinephelus flavocaeruleus*) grows up to 100 centimetres.*
Right *Nylon nets are easily made. Some are hundreds of metres long and the mesh sizes small; only small fish are able to slip through.*

more food is needed. The inhabitants of these frontier towns rely increasingly on marine products. Towns have sprung up near the Masoala Peninsula, from which fish and other marine products are processed and sold in the bigger centres of Antalaha and Maroantsetra and also in areas well beyond the region (sea cucumbers, for example, are exported to the Far East where, despite their rather unappetising appearance, they are greatly prized for their supposed aphrodisiac powers).

And there is yet another threat. Population growth means that more land has to be cleared for cattle grazing and rice production. Slash-and-burn farming techniques strip the land of its protective blanket, laying it bare, and when the rains come the valuable topsoil washes away, discolouring the once-pristine rivers. This silt finally reaches the lagoons, where it settles on and suffocates the reef. Mangroves (hardy vegetation with aerial roots) once acted as a buffer to these sediments, trapping the silt

brought down after tropical storms – but mangroves are now being harvested at a rapid rate for use as charcoal and, because the wood is strong and pliable, for construction. Large towns like Maroantsetra have virtually no mangroves left; the land around the river mouth has been given over to rice fields.

Inappropriate technology and too many people are posing a grievous threat to this fragile land. There is no clear solution, but ultimately the integrity of the environment

Left *A twobar clown fish (**Amphiprion allardi**) seeks security among the toxic tentacles of a sea anemone, its skin protected by a covering of mucus. In return for the safety the anemone provides, the fish will chase off other organisms that would otherwise prey on the anemone.*
Below *Octopuses are a popular seafood item the world over. However, new technology, such as masks, snorkels and spearguns, is allowing an even greater area of reef to be exploited by the villagers, even the deeper waters where life was once relatively safe.*

Below left *Market towns on the Masoala Peninsula offer many marine products to the town's inhabitants. With an average of ten children per family, even greater demands are now being placed on the protein resources of the ocean.*
Below right *Due to inappropriate netting techniques which break off coral heads when the net becomes trapped, the reef fish are rapidly lost and the coral heads destroyed, leaving the reef barren and lifeless. Such devastated areas will take many years to recover.*

depends on the people themselves, on their ability to recognise the dangers and their will to safeguard the future. Three small marine reserves have been declared on the Masoala Peninsula, and these may function as breeding areas that will restock those parts of the coast that lie between them. But the scheme's viability has yet to be tested. Meanwhile, the fisherfolk have no choice but to continue harvesting the diminishing resources. No one knows how much longer these resources can last.

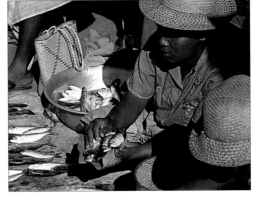

Living Laboratories

ISLANDS

Many islands of the southern subcontinental

region are showcases of natural selection – closed environments in which

evolution has often followed its own intriguing course.

Islands rank among the best venues for studying the earth's infinitely complex biological processes: they are 'living laboratories' in which adaptation and evolution have taken place in relatively secure isolation.

Not all islands are equally accessible though, and the chances of species settling on a specific island depend on the distance between the island and the mainland.

As a rule, the more remote the island the fewer species it supports, because the ocean acts as a barrier to distribution. Some life forms – birds, of course, and plants which depend on the wind for seed dispersal – are better equipped for colonisation than the more earth-bound species, whose ancestors invariably arrived on the scene by chance, carried across the sea by driftwood and other flotsam. Size is also a major factor: the larger the island, the greater the range of habitats and the wider the diversity of animals and plants.

THE MAGIC OF MADAGASCAR

About 165-million years ago the supercontinent of Gondwanaland began to break up, and one of its pieces – a large, 590 000 square kilometre chunk now known as Madagascar – drifted eastwards. Today the island is

Above *Gannets, terns and cormorants congregate in breeding colonies on Bird Island in Lambert's Bay.*

Left *When the Cape gannet arrives at its nesting site, it carries out a ritualised greeting display with its mate, called 'fencing'. During fencing, the pair bow heads together, tap bills and mutually groom each other to reaffirm their pair bond.*

Right *Many small islands along the southern African coast are free from natural predators and provide ideal nesting sites for coastal birds. Bird Island is one such island and is well-known for its large colonies of coastal birds, particularly Cape gannets.*

Cape Gannets

Cape gannets (Morus capensis) *breed on small islands along the west coast of South Africa and Namibia, such as Bird Island at Lambert's Bay* (overleaf). *These birds fly far offshore in search of food which consists of pilchards. After their long feeding excursions, nesting birds regurgitate their food* (right) *in response to the bill-pecking stimulus of their young. Immature birds are dark brown in colour with a speckled belly, but when fledged (usually during mid to late summer) they develop the striking white, black and yellow plumage of the adults. Populations of these sea birds, and of Cape cormorants* (Phalacrocorax capensis), *which also nest on Bird Island, have declined in recent years as increasingly they have been forced to compete with coastal fishing fleets for access to a limited food source.*

separated from its African parent by the 400-kilometre wide Mozambique Channel. This considerable gulf between the two, combined with the long period of separation, has allowed the process of evolution on Madagascar to follow its own, distinctive course.

Over millions of years plants and animals have managed, in one way or another, to cross the ever-widening divide, and to develop into a kaleidoscope of species, many of them unique. Although the island is equivalent to just two per cent of Africa's landmass it supports almost one-fifth of the continent's vascular plants, of which some 85 per cent are endemic to Madagascar. Orchids alone account for more than a thousand of its species, and animal groups – notably insects, snails, amphibians and reptiles – are equally diverse. Moreover, despite their mobility – their ability to migrate over long distances – more than 150 different types of bird breed only on the island.

LAND OF THE LEMURS

The stems of the large, succulent-like plant *Alluaudia procera* are covered in rows of formidable spines, but these don't deter Verreaux's sifaka, a lemur that nonchalantly leaps from tree to tree. The animal also has another means of locomotion: when the space between the trees is too large it crosses on foot, hopping along with its arms waving above its head (this helps it maintain balance). It has been known to travel as much as a 100 metres over the ground – behaviour that could only have evolved in a place where there are no large predators.

Scattered around Madagascar's coastal waters are other, smaller islands, among the best known of which is the densely forested Nosy Mangabe, located in the Baie d'Antongil in the northeastern region.

The islands support relatively abundant populations of five lemur species, including two endangered ones that have been introduced into what was considered a safe haven. Among them is the strange aye-aye (*Daubentonia madagascariensis*), the most elusive of them all, nocturnal and rarely seen. When feeding, it hooks grubs from the bark of trees with a long, skeletal, specially adapted finger, so occupying

Opposite, below *Many years ago Robben Island supported vast numbers of seals, penguins, gannets and terns. Today only a few species remain.*
Above *The surface of Ankarana is covered by limestone pinnacles known as* tsingy. *These rocky projections make movement across the surface difficult, particularly for larger creatures.*

an ecological niche that is usually filled by the woodpecker (of which there are none in Madagascar). Aye-ayes are highly endangered, not only because their habitat is disappearing but also because superstitious villagers, who fear them as harbingers of doom, hunt them to death. Two decades ago just 50 or so aye-ayes survived on the mainland, but in a last-ditch rescue effort some were captured and re-located to Nosy Mangabe, where they now appear to be flourishing.

Nosy Mangabe is also known for its leaf-tailed geckos, which flourish in the absence of such mainland predators as the civet-like fossa and the mongoose. The geckos' specialised disguise mechanism need only serve as a defence against the birds.

Because it is a small island on which the human presence can be efficiently regulated, and because it is a refuge for several rare species, Nosy Mangabe has been set aside as a nature reserve. The lemurs are easier to locate and observe here than they are elsewhere, and in fact many of the animals are becoming accustomed to visitors, which permits closer encounters with the wildlife. The island promises to become a prime eco-tourism destination. An additional attraction is a cave that has served as an ancestral tomb for families resident in the nearby mainland town of Maroantsetra.

Islands, though, need not be oceanic. Biologists consider an island as any area that is completely separated from similar countryside for geological, geographical or ecological reasons – and the definition covers inselbergs or rocky outcrops that occur the world over, from the forests of Madagascar to the Namib Desert. Inselberg literally means island-mountain, and in the Namib they sit above the great plains of gravel, pebbles and even the red dunes, isolated from other rocky patches by the wind-swept, shifting sands.

Many creatures have evolved features that adapt them to life in these lonely environments, among them the gecko. Two closely related gecko species of the genus *Rhoptropus* live on the Namib inselbergs near Gobabeb, and, like many members of the family, both have pads on the underside of their feet to help them climb the steep surfaces in their flight from predators. These lizards lay their eggs under flaking granite on overhanging rock faces, the young hatching in relative safety and sheltered from the sun. The geckos cannot easily move over the sandy terrain beyond their particular habitat, so one population is effectively isolated from others, even those of nearby inselbergs.

Some mountains also function as 'islands'. In northern Madagascar an expansive limestone escarpment, called Ankarana, rises above the surrounding savanna-like plains, its heights distinguished by sharp limestone pinnacles – known locally as *tsingy* (allegedly from the sound they make when struck) – that were formed over the ages by the processes of leaching and erosion. It is difficult to walk across the escarpment: the *tsingy* is sharp and it breaks

easily, and a journey of just a few 100 metres can take hours. Moreover, there are hollows below the surface, deep crevasses into which one can easily fall. The crowned lemur (*Lemur coronatus*), though, has little difficulty in negotiating this intimidating terrain, leaping with confident panache from pinnacle to pinnacle.

Ankarana has other claims to notability: it is pitted with caves and canyons, and in places the roof of the mountain has collapsed to create depressions that now sustain isolated patches of forest, each functioning as an isolated ecosystem. The caverns and their rivers are home to enormous eels and to crocodiles, some of which are reputed to be more than six metres long. Many of the caves have been charted; more are being explored.

THE GUANO ISLANDS

The classic image of a desert island, fringed by a few lonely palms and infinitely remote, does in fact fit many tropical atolls. Most are extremely dry, have no permanent surface water (hence their desert status) and in many cases no vegetation either, and they are profoundly inhospitable to most forms of life. But for some, they are a paradise. Free of predators, they serve as havens for breeding sea birds that are sometimes so abundant that their colonies cover the entire surface.

Southern Africa's south and west coasts have around forty such islands (though they tend to be close inshore, and not nearly so remote as their tropical counterparts), many of them are home to the jackass penguin (*Spheniscus demersus*), the only species of this flightless sea bird to breed in Africa. Jackass penguins are expert underwater swimmers, but they still need land on which to lay their eggs and rear their young – a legacy of their distant dinosaur ancestors. Other bird species also breed on these islands, among them cormorants, swift terns (*Sterna bergii*), Cape gannets – and Cape fur seals (*Arctocephalus pusillus*). Jutten and Malgas islands in Saldhana Bay, and Bird Island at Lambert's Bay further north, support especially large colonies. Since nesting sites are usually at a premium, there is a great deal of competition for space, and the islands have distinct areas where the different species congregate. Cape gannets, elegant birds with white

Opposite, left *There is a beautiful creek on Nosy Mangabe that ends in a picturesque waterfall that spills out from the forest over a beach. Among the local people, the creek has the reputation of having youth-restoring powers.*
Opposite, right above *The armoured chameleon is one of the many species that is unique to the island of Madagascar.*
Opposite, right below *On Nosy Mangabe isolated patches of lush tropical forest provide a safe refuge for many rare and endangered mainland species.*
Above *Several smaller islands are scattered around the coastal waters of Madagascar. Among the best known is Nosy Mangabe, an idyllic island paradise and a vital refuge for several rare species.*

Above The ring-tailed lemur (**Lemur catta**).
Left *Verreaux's sifaka (**Propithecus verreauxi
verreauxi**) has an alternative means of locomotion. When the distance between trees is too
large for these agile primates to cover in a jump,
they cross on foot, hopping along with their arms
waving above their heads. Such behaviour could
only have evolved in a place where there is no
threat from large predators.*
Opposite, left *About 20 years ago the aye-aye
was thought to be extinct. When new individuals
were discovered they were relocated to Nosy
Mangabe to protect them from the threats of the
mainland. This creature is the size of a small
monkey and has bat-like ears that can swivel
and pick up the slightest night sounds.*
Opposite, right *Although the baobab is a
familiar sight in southern Africa, eight of
the world's nine species of baobab are found
only in Madagascar.*

bodies, yellow heads, and black and blue trim-
ming, are among the most numerous. Both
the Cape gannet and the Cape cormorant feed
on the fish that live in the island's surrounding
waters. The cormorants have a fairly limited
feeding range, but gannets rove as far as
100 kilometres from their nesting sites in
search of food.

With so many birds feeding and nesting,
much of the guano – the droppings – finds its
way into the surrounding ocean to fertilise the
waters, creating productivity zones in a narrow
border around the island. Essential nutrients
are cycled through a system that begins with
guano and passes on to the kelp and other
marine algae that can take up nitrates from

the water. The algae supports marine herbivores and larger fish that, in turn, serve as a food supply for the sea birds.

TWO CONTRASTING ISLANDS

Madagascar, separated from mainland Africa millions of years ago, missed several important evolutionary events, the most significant of them the appearance of modern primates. Monkeys and apes spread throughout Africa and Asia, replacing the lemurs' ancestors in all places except this large Indian Ocean island.

The first modern primates to arrive in Madagascar were humans, who colonised the island about 1 500 years ago. Their influence on the environment, and that of the domestic animals they brought with them, has been nothing short of catastrophic – forests have been destroyed, untold numbers of species endangered, many driven to extinction, and large areas of land leached of topsoil. Yet, mirroring the evolutionary processes, the settlers took on a new identity during their isolation, developing a unique and distinct culture of tradition, custom, belief and life style.

Very different, much smaller, less isolated but, in some ways, with a similar environmental history is Robben Island in Cape Town's Table Bay. From early records, we know that it must have been an astonishing place: vast numbers of seals, penguins, cormorants, gannets, terns and many other sea birds once graced its pleasant shores. Within a few short years, though, most of these creatures had been clubbed, shot and eaten by hungry sailors after their long, dangerous journey along the west coast of southern Africa, where food and water

were notoriously scarce. Visiting ships' crews then started to leave sheep and other livestock on the island in an effort to create a renewable food source. Much of the natural life on the island was quickly destroyed as hungry animals grazed widely on the indigenous plants. Today the livestock has gone, but so has most of the indigenous flora.

Madagascar and Robben Island, like other islands of the world, are ecological microcosms of larger systems that operate in our biosphere. As natural wildernesses are threatened worldwide, soon all but the most inaccessible ecosystems will be reduced by human encroachment to scattered patches, fragile remnants of the earth's last remaining biological diversity.

Below *The large, bare surfaces of an inselberg aid in the accumulation of rain water at the base of the rocky outcrop, promoting the growth of plants that would otherwise struggle to survive on the dry plains and sand dunes of the Namib Desert.*

Right *Towering high above an otherwise unbroken landscape, the inselbergs of the Namib are an impressive spectacle.*

The Realm of Mankind

THE URBAN WORLD

In less than a million years the human race has spread itself

across the face of the planet, growing in numbers, in knowledge and in its ability

to control, to refashion and destroy the environment.

From its humble beginnings in the savanna of Africa a few million years ago, human life has proliferated throughout the globe. The highest mountain peaks have been tamed, the deepest ocean trenches explored, and a few men and women have even left the earth to probe the inner reaches of the solar system. From space and from the desolate plains of the moon, they have been able to look back at a planet now dominated by a single species, namely mankind.

The human population growth on planet Earth, however, has not been a steady progression: there have been three major behavioral revolutions along the bumpy road from the time the world first accommodated just a few hundred thousand people to today's vast melting pot of approximately five billion individuals.

A fourth revolution might very well be imminent. *Homo sapiens* lords over the planet, displaying contempt for all other forms of life, and is even threatening his own existence, monopolising and voraciously consuming the earth's biological resources, diverting and damming its life-giving rivers, mining its rocks and precious metals at a rapacious and alarming rate, and even changing its atmosphere.

THE INTELLIGENT APE

The advent of tool-making was probably the most important step in mankind's rise to dominance. With a vastly more productive capability to feed and protect themselves, humanoids grew in numbers and began to

Above *Much of southern Africa's natural pasture has been sacrificed for consumption of cereal crops such as wheat.*
Left *European colonists brought many alien species with them, such as the North American grey squirrel (**Sciurus carolinensis**).*
Right *The city of Cape Town is just 300 years old. Throughout the industrialised world, expanding cities, jewelled with light, illuminate night skies.*

Top *In the Western Cape the blue crane* (**Anthropoides paradisea**) *must share its traditional grazing area with domestic livestock.* **Above** *Rock martins* (**Hirundo fuligula**) *hatch their young in a nest built from mud pellets, nestled in a corner of a building under the eaves.*

spread outwards from their African evolutionary cradle. More sophisticated tool-making techniques, perhaps coupled with the evolu-

tion of language approximately 10 000 years ago, culminated in the introduction of agriculture. For the first time, crops were cultivated and animals domesticated for food and transport, creating surpluses, commercial trade and specialisation, and a surging human population. Even during the earliest civilisations, people were beginning to change the landscape. Forests were felled for building materials and firewood, and the soil planted with new crops; rivers were dammed and diverted for irrigation to produce even more food. Time to think, discuss and invent heralded the dawn of a new age, and the next expansion in numbers.

More and more land was swallowed up; improved transport forged links between distant communities, and widespread trade and commerce provided the building blocks of great empires. Then, having improved ways to produce and store food, and having devised a scientific approach to medicine and disease, mankind broke free of all the world's natural constraints. The Industrial Revolution of the

last century, the formalisation of knowledge into scientific thought, and the advances in technology, have led to some of man's finest achievements. Only recently has the world community recognised the price that has been paid: the damage done to our planet.

A PLANET IN CRISIS

Today, most people live in a world almost entirely of their own making. They travel on roads that carve sterile paths across the land, and walk in concrete jungles devoid of life. Among the vastly diverse habitats supported by the biosphere, a new biome must now be recognised – the realm of man, an ecosystem with the city as its nucleus, man's largest communal arena of activity and cooperation. In these cities people are born and reared; here they reproduce and die, their bodies disposed of in the manner dictated by religion, custom and personal preference, be it buried, burnt or placed on a raft to drift down the Ganges River to eternity. The great cities are not independent of that world: in order to feed these dense, energy-consuming citadels of human enterprise, vast swathes of land are dedicated to their needs.

In these agricultural environments nature is harnessed and given over to monocultures of specially bred cereal crops. Technology and improved farming methods have led to huge rises in food production. Between 1969 and 1989 world cereal output doubled; over the same period, population numbers rose by only two-thirds. Even so, more and more people are forced to accept hunger as a way of life. Storage and distribution are the main problems, but, given the political will and proper organisation, a large part of the world can be adequately fed.

But the question remains: 'How long can this growth continue?' Limits are being reached in many areas, while poor agricultural practices in others are seriously reducing the productivity of the land. Rapidly rising populations, particularly in the developing world, are an ominous prelude to the day of reckoning.

Water, the single most precious resource in southern Africa, is being monopolised for agriculture, mining, industry and domestic use. Vast numbers of pipes are plumbed into the city network for water supply and waste disposal, cables for energy transmission and, increasingly, communication. There now seems very little room for the natural world. Yet, animals and plants do survive and even flourish: gardens and parks are havens for birds, insects and other creatures that have adapted to urban life; pigeons and starlings find roosting sites in the inner areas on city buildings; while on the ground, rats, mice, cockroaches and a myriad invertebrates thrive as they have always done.

Even some birds of prey have benefited from the growth of civilisation, occasionally finding food resources more plentiful than in the wild. Kestrels, for instance, can often be seen hunting along roadsides in both Europe and southern Africa. Here, the vegetation is free from the larger herbivores and insects flourish. But the fast-moving traffic creates a high roadside mortality rate among insects, which support small mammal populations that, in turn, sustain the avian predators which have learnt to hunt in this new, busy environment. Meanwhile, in the agricultural lands, cattle egrets (*Bubulcus ibis*) follow domestic livestock as they graze, perpetuating an ancient natural cycle in which buffalo were once their partners. Adaptation to human activity is posing new threats: indiscriminate use of pesticides and herbicides has led to drug resistance, most notably among some malaria strains. If new preventative drugs are not developed, and properly implemented, once again malaria could become the scourge of mankind.

INTO THE NEXT MILLENNIUM

Since the advent of agriculture 10 000 years ago, humans have wiped out forests equivalent in area to more than half the land surface of the African continent. Each year, more water than is contained in the whole of East Africa's Lake Victoria is diverted for human consumption. Urbanisation in southern Africa is increasing at a rate equal to that of any other country in the developing world: over a quarter of South Africa's population now lives in towns and cities, and by the year 2010 this figure will probably have doubled, placing demands on the subcontinent's resources that even now cannot be met. If present patterns of consumption continue, water resources in the Western Cape will not be able to sustain Cape Town in just a few decades time.

Right *Despite a decrease in their numbers, vervet monkeys (**Cercopithecus aethiops**) have found new and innovative ways to survive among humankind and technology.*

Opposite *While extravagant homes continue to be built along the coast, most of the subregion's population lives below the poverty line; many still face hunger and poverty in times of drought.* **Above** *The slopes of Table Mountain are under threat from urban development and alien species.* **Left** *Oil spills have a profound impact on coastal marine life; sea birds are often the first to suffer.*

If we are to deal with the crises planet Earth will face in the twenty-first century, we shall need a new framework for managing the human race on a global scale. A new identity in the natural world must be defined. Due to vastly growing numbers and to the complexity of society, mankind has taken on a collective character reminiscent of Earth's most socially organised animals, the insects; human communities are like the hives and colonies of ants, bees, termites and wasps – concentrations of life in which communication and the division of labour enable their members to accomplish great feats of engineering, and to create whatever kind of environment they aspire to.

The social implications of this scenario are difficult to assess. In the past, people lived in close-knit communities where personal encounter was part of daily life, and cooperation vital to individual and collective preservation, reciprocal acts of kindness and help essential to survival, with little latitude afforded to those who broke the rules. In the mass anonymity of cities today, such encounters are so infrequent that the moral structures, around which much of our society was once woven, no longer apply. The result: a dog-eat-dog dynamic and an escalation in crime that threatens to destroy social structures from within. Governments and their control mechanisms – the civil administration, armed forces and police – now seem unable to cope in the rapidly changing social arena.

Beyond the cities loom even greater threats to our survival, with scientists predicting widespread environmental catastrophe on all fronts: soil erosion, pollution, acid rain, oil spills, a weakening ozone layer and global warming. In the final analysis, questions regarding our future will have to be phrased in simple ecological terms. How long can human numbers keep increasing? Are we facing a global Armageddon of our own making, with social breakdown from within and environmental degradation beyond?

There seems to be two possible scenarios for the future. One is that the rising prices of natural resources will curb consumption which will encourage conservation and lead to more efficient ways of occupying our world. Already such trends can be perceived, for instance in the increasing emphasis on recycling.

Despite such glimmers of hope, the pace of change may simply be too rapid, and the second scenario paints a much bleaker picture. By the middle of the next century, demands on resources that are already stretched to their limits will force radical changes in social priorities and in the way people live their lives. Humankind's legendary ability to adjust behaviour to meet the demands of a changing natural world has always been its salvation, but the prognosis for life on earth looks grim.

Various fundamental trends can be identified. First, overpopulation is one of the great threats: the developed world's way of life is as great a threat to the global ecosystem as the Third World's population growth. Second, a

Top *Increasingly, one sees human development alongside the natural world. Flamingos thrive in waters around the New Brighton township in Port Elizabeth.*

Above *Most of what man casually throws away can damage the environment in some way. A Cape gannet, with an abandoned net wrapped tightly around its beak, died from starvation.*

world society has evolved in which people eat, burn, buy and live as if there are no limits to the planet's resources. The message is simple: more is better. Consumerism is no longer confined to Western civilization: it is spreading like a disease through every society.

Third, there is a general reluctance to do away with inappropriate technologies, many of which have caused or will cause ecological disasters, of which the Chernobyl nuclear meltdown, massive oil spills, and the exhausting of key, non-renewable resources are prominent examples. There are also problems at a more fundamental level. In Madagascar, slash-and-burn agriculture and over-exploitation of tropical fish stocks through the use of small-gauge nylon nets exemplify the inappropriate use of technology throughout the developing world. At one level, a switch to ecologically sensitive and sometimes more primitive farming methods with lower, but more sustainable, returns is needed. At another level, new technologies such as solar power, wind power, even an alter-

Above and right *The motor industry is one of the greatest consumers of natural resources on the planet: vast areas of land are lost to road networks, and precious fossil fuels will soon be exhausted .*

native to the inefficient internal combustion engine, need to be employed despite their short-term development costs. Thus the principal question of our time remains: can we, as a species, meet such formidable challenges during the next hundred years? Planet Earth is humankind's own island in the barren void of space, and its limits will be reached.

Ultimately a new balance will be found, either by man himself or as the result of some cataclysmic social or ecological occurence. Even without humans, many life forms on Earth are likely to continue until the sun finally begins to dim, and our mark in the annals of a planet already four-and-a-half-billion years old may turn out to be just a tiny scratch.

Further Reading

Evolution and Ecology

Adams, D. & Carwardine, M. 1991. *Last Chance to See* Pan, London.

Dawkins, R. 1990. *The Blind Watchmaker* Penguin, London.

Gould, S.J. 1982. *Ever since Darwin* Penguin, Middlesex.

Marine Life

Branch, G.M., Griffiths, C.L., Branch, M.L. & Beckley, L.E. 1994. *Two Oceans – A Guide to the Marine Life of Southern Africa* David Philip, Cape Town & Johannesburg.

Branch, M.& G. 1981. *The Living Shores of Southern Africa* Struik, Cape Town.

Debelius, H. 1993. *Indian Ocean Tropical Fish Guide* Aquaprint, Germany.

King, D. 1996. *Reef Fishes and Corals – East Coast of Southern Africa* Struik, Cape Town.

The Arid Lands

Johnson, P. & Bannister, A. 1993. *Namibia: Africa's Harsh Paradise* Struik, Cape Town.

Lovegrove, B. 1993. *The Living Deserts of Southern Africa* Fernwood Press, Cape Town.

The Okavango

Johnson, P. & Bannister, A. 1993. *Sea of Land – Land of Water* Struik, Cape Town.

Madagascar

Preston-Mafham, K. 1991. *Madagascar – A Natural History* Struik, Cape Town.

Savanna & Bushveld

Dennis, N. & Scholes, B. 1995. *The Kruger Park - Wonders of an African Eden* Struik, Cape Town.

Fynbos

Cowling, R. & Richardson, D. 1995. *Fynbos – South Africa's Unique Floral Kingdom* Fernwood Press, Cape Town.

General Southern African Natural History

Branch, 1994. *Field Guide to Snakes and other Reptiles of Southern Africa* Struik, Cape Town.

Duggan, A. (ed.) Readers Digest 1983 *Game Parks and Nature Reserves of Southern Africa* Readers Digest, Cape Town

Sinclair, I., Hockey, P. & Tarboton, W. 1995. *Sasol Birds of Southern Africa* Struik, Cape Town.

Skaife, S.H. 1994. *African Insect Life* Struik, Cape Town.

Smithers, R.H.N. & Skinner, J.D. 1990. *The Mammals of the Southern African Subregion* University of Pretoria, Pretoria.

Photographic Credits

SIL= Struik Image Library; **ABPL=** Anthony Bannister Photo Library

Adrian Bailey: pp 88, 90; **Anthony Bannister:** p 93; **Anthony Bannister/ABPL:** pp 96, 100 (bottom left); **Daryl Balfour:** pp 48 (top), 51, 61, 78 (bottom), 81 (top right), 84 (top left), 89 (top), 92, 94, 97, 98, 100 (top left, right, and bottom right), back cover (bottom left), half title page, title page; **Peter Best/SA Museum:** p 63 (bottom right); **Marlies Bohm:** p 132 (bottom); **Cape Town Electricity Photographic Studio:** pp 124 (bottom), 137; **Gerald Cubitt:** pp 23, 35 (top right), 83, 129 (left), 131; **Roger de la Harpe/SIL:** pp 38 (top and bottom), 65; **Nigel Dennis:** pp 77, 79, 82 (bottom), 101, 104, 105, 109 (bottom), 111, 126 (top right), 128 (right); **Nigel Dennis/ABPL:** p 81 (bottom right); **Nigel Dennis/SIL:** pp 12 (top), 14 (right), 43 (top), 72, 76, contents page, 78 (top), 85 (left), 86, 87, 95, 106 (left), 128 (left); **Gerhard Dreyer/SIL:** p 20 (top); **Gerhard Dreyer:** pp 24 (bottom), 64 (top), 68, 70 (top), 132 (top); **C Friend/SIL:** p 91 (bottom); **Albert Froneman:** p 15; **Brenton Geach/The Argus:** p 63(top); **Lex Hes/Photo Access:** p 64 (bottom); **Lex Hes:** p 74; **Gerald Hinde/ABPL:** p 73; **Leonard Hoffman/SIL:** pp 35 (bottom right), 40 (bottom); **Luc Hosten/Landmarks:** p 138; **Dennis King:** pp 113, 114, 115, 116 (left), 117 (bottom), 118, 119 (left), 120, back cover (bottom right); **Department of Water and Forestry Knysna:** p 25 (top); **Walter Knirr/SIL:** pp 13, 136; **NPH Photography/Photo Access:** p 16; **François Odendaal:** pp 59 (bottom), 103, 125; **Colin Paterson-Jones:** pp 26 (bottom), 29 (top), 41, 44 (top), 45 (top), 46 (bottom left and right), 47; 48 (bottom), 49 (bottom), 85 (right), 89 (bottom) 134, back cover (top left); **Anton Pauw:** pp 12 (bottom), 14 (top and bottom left), 28 (top), 75 (left), 81 (bottom left), 82 (top), 84 (bottom left), 99, 130 (left); **Charl Pauw:** p 19 (top); **Pennington's Butterfly Trust:** p 20 (bottom); **Doug Perrine:** Planet Earth/Photo Access: p 39; **Peter Pickford/SIL:** p 17 (bottom), 49 (top), 91 (top), 135; **Peter Pinnock:** p 117 (top); **Herman Potgieter:** pp 123, 139 (bottom); **Alain Proust:** p 137 (top); **SA Museum:** p 19 (bottom); **Inge Schubert:** front flap; **Mark Skinner:** pp 39 (top), 133; **Lorna Stanton/ABPL:** p 18; **A J Stevens/Photo Access:** p 84 (bottom right); **Peter Steyn/Photo Access:** p 17 (top); **Erhart Thiel/SIL:** p 70; **Hein van Hörsten/SIL:** pp 52, 54; **Lanz van Hörsten/SIL:** pp 75, 80; **Claudio Velasquez:** pp 22 (left), 24 (top), 25 (bottom), 26 (top), 27, back flap, front cover, back cover (top right), spine, preface, 28 (bottom), 29 (bottom), 30 (top), 32-34, 35 (left), 36, 37, 40 (top), 42, 43 (bottom), 44 (bottom), 43 (bottom), 46 (top and middle), 51, 53, 54 (top and bottom left), 55-58, 59 (top left and right), 60-62, 63 (bottom left), 66-67, 69, 102, 106 (right), 107, 108, 109 (top), 110, 112, 119 (right), 121-122, 124 (top and middle), 126 (left and bottom right), 127; **Paul Wagner/Photo Access/Getaway:** p 129 (right); **Zelda Wahl:** p 139 (top).

Index